G 3/96

Thai Literature

Thai Literature
An Introduction

Klaus Wenk

Translated from the German by
Erich W. Reinhold

© 1995, Klaus Wenk. All rights reserved.

White Lotus Co., Ltd
G.P.O. Box 1141
Bangkok 10501

Published 1995. First Edition

Printed in Thailand

Typeset by COMSET Limited, Partnership

ISBN 974-8496-33-3   pbk.   White Lotus Co., Ltd.; Bangkok
ISBN 1-879155-48-6   pbk.   White Lotus Co., Ltd.; Cheney

Contents

Preface	vii
The Sukhothai Period	1
The Literature of the Ayutthaya Period	6
The Thonburi Period	27
The Bangkok Period	28
The Literature of the Present	78
Bibliography	115
Index	118

Preface

The present survey of Thai literature aims at giving all those interested in the culture of Thailand an opportunity to inform themselves, in terms easy to comprehend, about the extensive and varied writings that have been passed down over the last seven hundred years. The survey does not claim to comprise all titles and dates of literary relevance, but it contains all that is essential. If some parts have been stressed more than others, this is accounted for by the author's predilection for certain poets. Broader space and a more detailed description has been given to all subjects that the author considers to be typical and of peculiar interest to the western reader. In this context it must be pointed out that the literature of the Thai is to a large extent still unexplored. It is hence appropriate to make reservations in presenting certain facts and findings. Also, it is worth noting that C and c as initials are pronounced djo (จ). Those interested in more detailed information on specific subjects may refer to the bibliography at the end of the book. Only those titles which are easily accessible have been listed. May this study contribute towards facilitating the approach to, and the understanding of, the complex culture of a country which has, only too often, been summarily dealt with in cliché phrases.

Hamburg 1995, Klaus Wenk

The Sukhothai Period, 1250–1350

In the West little has hitherto been known about Thai literature. It is only over the last thirty years or so that the literature of the Thai people has come to the attention of oriental studies the world over. In sharp contrast to this, the literature of some other non-European cultures has been the subject of intense study and research over a period of two hundred years. So far, only a few classical Thai literary works—in flawless translations—are available to the general reader.

But even to the native Thai a good part of their literature is yet *terra incognita*. A great number of poetical works have not yet even been printed and many hundreds are known to only scholars and orientalists who have access to manuscripts in the National Museum in Bangkok. Much philological controversy and literary criticism centers around the poetical works which are available in print. Many have been destroyed with the passage of time—this fact is clearly documented by source references in the case of legal texts and commentaries. Consequently, all surveys of Thai literature must necessarily be fragmentary for the time being. In the following chapters the division into literary periods is tentative and not based on dictates imposed by literary history. The division into periods adopted here runs parallel to the timing of general history. Surely, a great deal of further scholarly effort will be called for before the periods of Thai literature can be determined with validity.

The origins of the literature of the Thai people is unknown. A fixed date can be assigned only to the first literary document that has been handed down to us, an inscription on a stele, about one metre in height, which **Khun Ram Kamhaeng**—King of Sukhothai—ordered to be erected in the year 1292. All events and reports prior to this could at best be dated hypothetically or by conjecture.

Thai Literature

The inscription on the stele, which marks the beginning of recorded Thai literature, is couched in pleasant-sounding terse language in which Ram Kamhaeng gives an account of his family, his deeds and the state of his realm. The brief sentences arranged in rhythmic patterns are made up for the most part by monosyllabic and frequently alliterative words. 'In the water is fish, in the fields is rice. . . .'

We may presume that the oldest poem stemming from the Sukhothai period is the collection of proverbs known as *Suphasit Phra Ruong*. These proverbs mark the beginning of a literary genre that prospered right into the twentieth century. Didactic and occasionally moralizing verses are typical of a cultural community that strove to follow the 'middle path' in every respect and to keep the mind calm and composed. There is a collection of these proverbs, some of them perhaps invented aphorisms which are loosely, if at all, connected. In the main they contain practical rules for coping with everyday life. Many of them are less attractive from a purely literary point of view.

The best known work of this period and the most significant with regard to its content is the *Traiphumikhatha*, a 'treatise on the three worlds' which was commissioned, as is generally assumed, by the Sukhothai ruler Lithai in the year 1345. That the king himself could have been the author, an assumption frequently made, is implausible. It is one of the oldest treatise on Buddhist cosmology known thus far. The three worlds do not represent the earthly, the infernal and the heavenly spheres, as is generally supposed, but the three Buddhist forms of existence of the sentient world, i.e., the world of the five senses, *kama-loka*; the corporeal world of the sixteen celestial grades or *rupa-loka*; and the incorporeal world or *arupa-loka* in which the five senses are no longer operative. In particular, the various forms of punishment suffered by sinners in the primary and secondary hells are described in great detail.

The account brings home to the reader that there are obviously no limits to human imagination in inventing all sorts of cruelties. The celestial amenities, on the other hand, are described in rather sober and unimaginative language. The diction of this treatise is refined and stylized as appropriate to the subject-matter. The Thai language is interspersed with foreign words from Pali, Sanskrit and Cambodian.

Excerpts from *Traiphumikhatha*

(Chapter I)
The Major Hells, Auxiliary Hells, and *Lokhanta* Hells

The Sukhothai Period, 1250–1350

Beings who commit sins with their bodies, mouths and minds will be reborn in the four realms of destruction and suffering, especially in the eight major hells . . . These are located underneath the world we live in, one below the other. The hell known as 'hell of suffering without reprieve' is on the lowest level. The hell known as 'hell of those killed but invariably brought back to life' live for five hundred hellish years. In this hell a single day and a night equals 9,000,000 years in the human world . . . The eight major hells have four corners with gates at the four main points of access. The floors of these hells are paved with glowing red iron, likewise the ceilings covering them are of glowing red iron . . . These hells are full of beings crammed together. The fire never goes out, it burns until the end of the aeon . . . The eight major hells are surrounded by sixteen auxiliary hells on each side . . .

(Chapter 5)
The Realm of Men.

Birth from a Human Womb.

Beings born in the realm of men are born in one of the four modes. Three modes occur occasionally, however, birth from the human womb is by far the most common. The following process goes on in the womb that bears the person to be born and reborn. Women who are young and ought to have children carry a clod of thick blood in the lower part of their abdomen. When a child is about to be born, the ever increasing clod turns red like a vine berry called *plang*. The seven days subsequent to menstruation, when the blood flows out of the womb, is the period during which the baby is born or reborn. From that time onwards the usual menstrual flow ceases altogether.

All women who are not old should bear children. The reason why some women do not bear children must be attributed to the effects of former bad deeds of those to be born; the evil deeds cause winds to swirl in the woman's abdomen, swaying the embryo to and fro, smiting it so it cannot develop and dies. . . .

Among human beings three kinds of children are born. The first kind is called children of 'superior status', the second, children of 'similar status', and the third, 'children of inferior status' . . . There are four kinds of human beings. One kind is known as men equaling infernal beings, another is known as men equaling suffering ghosts, another as men equaling animals, and still another as men completely human. Of the latter there are again four groups . . . (The chapter on the human realm rambles on in this strain for about a hundred pages.)

3

Thai Literature

(Chapter 6)
The Realm of the Gods.

Now follows a description of the gods who are born in the six realms of sensual desire. One kind depicts the gods who exist by general assent; another portrays gods by dint of birth; and a third by dint of purity. The rulers and kings of our land who are familiar with the fundamental principles, who know the dhamma, and act according to the ten dhammic rules for kings, are called gods by dint of general assent. Those in the six upper realms of sensual desire in the celestial sphere which reaches upwards to the Brahma world are called gods by dint of birth. Buddha, Pacceka Buddha, the enlightened one, the holy saints whose senses are free from delusions, and Buddha's disciples, i.e., those having entered Nibbana are called gods by dint of purity.

(Chapter 10)
The End of the World Aeon (Mahakappa).

The Cosmic Destruction.

Sentient beings having consciousness and being born in the thirty-one realms are transitory and pass away since the ruler of death brings about their end.
When the fire flares up to destroy the aeon ... what will it be like? The conflagration and total destruction of the aeon can be brought about by each of three efficient forces. One of these is fire, another water, and still another wind ... In the process of conflagration all eleven levels of the world of sensual desires are consumed.

(Chapter 11)
Nibbana and the Paths.

The Kinds of Nibbana

The treasures of Nibbana are a very high degree of joy, happiness and calm. There is nothing on earth comparable to these treasures. If you combine the treasures of Indra and the brahma and compare them with Nibbana, it is like comparing a fire-fly with the moon or, in other words, like a drop of water at the end of a strand of hair compared with the water of an ocean of unfathomable depths ...

The Sukhothai Period, 1250–1350

There are two kinds of Nibbana attained by those who have completely freed themselves from the host of defilements. One kind is known as Nibbana with a trace of the substance of life remaining, the other is known as Nibbana with no trace of the life substance remaining ... There are eight paths leading to Nibbana. Who are those dignified beings who tread these paths? Everyone who has got rid of the three hundred kinds of defilement will reach the path of those who enter the stream ... Those who have got rid of another four hundred defilements, in addition to the three hundred defilements which they got rid of previously, will reach the path known as the 'heavenly path' which is the path of no rebirth and they will enjoy the bliss of never being born again.

According to tradition another literary work is assigned to the Sukhothai period: the poem *Nang Nophamat* (the Dame Nophamat). The text available in print today, however, cannot possibly be the original text of the fourteenth or fifteenth century. The idiom of the printed text points to a considerably later period. On the other hand, it is quite plausible that the poem was composed rather early and re-edited during a later period. Nang Nophamat is said to have been a lady of the court of King Lithai who reigned from 1354 until 1376. As is typical of all poetry of ancient Thailand, the poem begins with a eulogy of the King. This, however, cannot be interpreted in present-day terminology as proving a state of dependency of the poet. In the patriarchal monarchy of ancient Thailand there still existed an unbroken relationship between the ruler and the ruled. It was customary to pay reverence to the higher ranking person, because in Buddhist understanding he had acquired a greater degree of 'merit.'

The poem further describes court-life, popular customs, traditions, and festivals. Last but not least, instructions are given for the accepted behavior of a lady-in-waiting. Admittedly, some of the verses are quite attractive poetically, however, by and large, the poem today has historic value only in the cultural and literary spheres.

Apart from the works mentioned there exists a great number of inscriptions on steles and on the bases of Buddha images. However, these inscriptions are of greater significance for general history, and the history of art and linguistics than for the history of literature.

The Literature of the Ayutthaya Period, 1350–1767

The beginning of the history of the literature of the Ayutthaya period is commonly believed to coincide with the beginning of the general history of Ayutthaya. This, however, is not altogether true. For at least a century cultural activities went on simultaneously in Sukhothai and the chief residential cities of the rising state of Ayutthaya.

Only a fragment of the literary production of the first two centuries of the Ayutthaya period has come down to us. The reason for this must be sought, on the one hand, in the fortuity of what has been preserved at all and, on the other, in the fact that the residential centers of a realm that was intent on conquest and subsequent military rule were, in their early stages, no seats of the muses.

A text preserved from the beginning of the dynasty and titled *Ong kan chaeng nam*, roughly rendered as 'Royal Oath on Water' exists. This, however, is of greater interest to the cultural rather than to the literary historian. It is a cycle of verses recited by court Brahmins on the occasion of military officers and civil servants swearing the oath of allegiance. Before the oath was actually taken, the royal weapons were immersed in holy water which was afterwards drunk by the oath-takers. During the ceremony the Brahmins recited verses threatening the potential oath-breaker with curse and punishment.

The literary production of the Ayutthaya period extends over several centuries and is connected above all with the names of three rulers whose reign enhanced not only its political but also its cultural position, viz., **Trailokhanat**, 1488–88; **Narai**, 1657–88; and **Boromakot**, 1735–58.

Trailokhanat's victory over the northern Thai principality of Chieng Mai was dealt with in the epic poem *Yuon Phai*, the 'Vanquished Yuon' (Yuon is synony-

The Literature of the Ayutthaya Period, 1350–1767

mous with northern Thai). Linguistically, this epic is one of the most complex texts preserved.

It is assumed that King Trailokhanat was also responsible for the composition of the poem *Thet Mahachat* or ' The Great Divine Rebirth', a work of Buddhist inspiration. The text is based on Jataka No. 547, the *Vessantara Jataka*, or the last of the canon and occupies a prominent place in Thai Buddhism and hence also in art and literature.

Of greater poetic significance, however, is the *Lilit Phra Lo*, a poem written in a metre called *lilit* which combines verse with rhythmic prose. The plot is probably based on a real event, but the artistic arrangement of the poem was inspired by the muses. The verses relate the love and death of the splendid hero Phra Lo. Two princesses of a neighboring hostile realm fall in love with the royal prince who was transported to them by magic. Together they share their love, lust and pleasure; but, their happy state is thwarted by a female ancestor of the princesses. She orders the guards to take Phra Lo prisoner in order to sentence him to death. The lovers, however, are resolved to defy all forces that might separate them and eventually fall to their death in a battle against superior enemy forces.

Lilit Phra Lo is the first specimen of belletristic literature in Thailand in which free rein is given to imagination, belief in miracles and things unreal. It is also the first love-story known of in Thai literature. In subsequent centuries many more followed. Henceforth, works of edification, diversion and entertainment were added to the more or less factual literature of the past. It is not known who the author of *Lilit Phra Lo* was.

No significant literary works of the ensuing years have been preserved. For sometime literature of a more functional nature was produced. It was during the reign of Trailokhanat that the first constitutional laws were promulgated. These laws concerned the hierarchical structure of ancient Thai society, the rights of the nobility, the administration of the country, and the important state ceremonies. Procedural law and parts of substantive criminal and civil law were dealt with in great detail. Buddhist treatises in Thai or Pali were written in that epoch and one can safely assume that even chronicles were compiled but have not been handed down to us.

Thai literary historians consider the reign of Phra Narai to be the 'Golden Age' of Thai indigenous literature. The king himself was held to be a poet of repute and reports claim that the poetic elite gathered at his court. It was during this period that the four-line *khlong* metre, especially suited for aphorisms, came into vogue.

Thai Literature

The story goes that King Narai is said to have recited one or two verse lines to a courtier and expected him to complete the poem in a witty and concise manner. Apart from the King, only four other poets who belonged to the King's home of the muses are known to us:
Maharatchakhru, the 'great royal teacher'
Phra Horathibodi, the 'court astrologer'
Si Mahosot
Si Prat
Si Prat was the youngest and also the most renowned of the four. The most lyrical poem of ancient Thailand, the *Khlong Kamsuon Si Prat* and the epic poem *Anirut kham chan* are among others ascribed to him. *Kamsuon Si Prat* or 'Si Prat's Complaint' is one of the first and most outstanding specimens of the *nirat*, a genre often recurring in Thai literature. The word may be rendered rather inadequately as ' Farewell Poem'. The poet expresses his longing for his far-away beloved by giving an account of his travels mostly in broad epic language. Few poets were able to avoid banality in this genre. Si Prat, however, succeeded.

His second poem *Anirut*, a work of significant length, is based on a tale from the Puranas in which a love-story is fabulously arranged. Anirut, a grandson of Krishna, is transported to princess Usha by a tree goddess. He is, however, taken back to his homeland after their first night of love. Driven by longing Usha tries to find out who her lover is. By magic she succeeds in leading Anirut back to her. However, Usha's father who disapproves of the love affair thwarts the relationship, but eventually the story has a happy ending through the intervention of Krishna.

As is typical of most poems of this period, this poem begins in solemn fashion by praising the glory of the gods and their abodes:
(1) There was a time when the noble discus bearer was transformed into Lord Krishna who fought against suffering; hostile princes and opponents prostrated before him.
(2) He revealed himself and made his abode the city of Dvaravati which excelled even the realm of Vishnu in splendor.
(3) Its walls covered with crystals, heavenly gold, and sparkling jewels outshone the brightness of the sun.
(4) Heaven and earth were aglow with pure light of celestial brightness, shining day and night.
(5) Gods and demons filled with joy lauded and praised the supreme Lord of the earth.

The Literature of the Ayutthaya Period, 1350–1767

(6) On top of the jewel-bedecked walls were rows of serrated edges so sharp as to cut the wind.
(7) The city was as high as the abode of Brahma. It was admired by heaven and earth. Even the abode of Indra was no match for it.
(8) There was shining light in the main hall with its triple porch studded with crystals mixed with gold and sparkling jewels. There was not the like of it anywhere.
(9) The city was surrounded by three lines of fortifications embracing it like three huge arms. Enemies found it difficult to overcome. Any attempt would be doomed to failure.
(10) They did not dare to attack. Even the demons were discouraged and kept away from it.
(11) There were sunshades and banners of victory installed on the ramparts of the triple line of defense elaborately decorated with crystals
(12) resembling the disc of the sun and the moon. They protected the city and provided shade.
(13) There were buildings bedecked with glittering gold, their walls covered all over with floral ornaments and decorated with jewels—a magnificent view to behold.
(14) Men on earth and the gods in Shiva's world were likewise delighted by it.

Si Prat's personal destiny was akin to that of other highly gifted poets with a witty and mocking disposition who found it difficult to conform to court etiquette. A love-affair with a lady of the 'inner palace' led to his banishment to Nakhon Si Thamarat in Southern Thailand. The story of his life soon became legendary.

It is reported that the poet made friends with the local governor. This soon paved the way for him to become the central figure from among a circle of poets. However, another love-affair blossomed between himself and a minor wife of the governor. Cutting short legal proceedings Si Prat was sentenced to death and decapitated. He is said to have composed the following verse in protest but, at the same time, in resignation to his fate:

Goddess of the earth look down upon me   with your penetrating eye.
I am the son of a sage   I am quite somebody!
If I did wrong, well he may kill me   I shall gladly suffer it.
If, however, I did no wrong, and he
  still kills me   this sword shall repay him for
     his evil deed.

Maharatchakhru is known above all as the author of *Samuthakhot kham chan*, a poem which he did not finish. The King is said to have personally added another part to the work after the poet's death. The poem was not completed until the Bangkok period in the year 1849. *Samuthakhot* too is based on a love-story, similar in its motifs to Anirut, from which it was presumably derived. Maharatchakhru's second poem Sua Kho, 'The Tiger and the Calf', is written in a similar strain with its motifs borrowed from Indian fairy-tales: A tiger cub made friends with a calf. Both went to an hermit who transformed them by giving them human forms. Through their heroic deeds each of them won a royal princess as a wife. The lovers were, however, separated through intrigues and bad luck. Eventually, there was a happy reunion but not before they had braved many dangers and adventures.

With the three verse poems *Anirut*, *Samuthakhot*, and *Sua Kho* the Thai *belles-lettres* was firmly established for some generations to come. From then on the content of these themes, arranged in fairy-tale fashion, did not gain in depth. There were also a number of poems written in difficult to comprehend elevated language with the inclusion of foreign words borrowed from Cambodian, Lao and Pali. Nevertheless, poetry was not altogether relegated to the level of trashy literature. During that epoch the metre of the poems changed, but their euphony remained captivating. The plot structure was invariably the same: an illustrious hero wins the heart of a fair lady. The couple are then separated, in most cases by events for which they are themselves responsible. They are eventually reunited, through the intervention of gods bestowed with magical attributes, but not before having overcome numerous obstacles.

Literature of this kind is scarcely of any interest to the contemporary reader who, unable to understand Thai, cannot hope to savor the study and analysis of difficult philological problems and obsolete vocabulary. The rhythm of the narrative is heavy, the diction bare and unadorned like that of officious documents. The exaggerated passion for detail has a trifling effect.

The following are examples by which the reader may judge for himself:
- (96) The mobile troops were equipped with golden chariots with five-colored flags set with glittering precious stones.
- (97) The mobile troops had beautiful chariots with long pennants. The officers were armed with bows.
- (98) The mobile troops had chariots that went to battle, drawn by daring lions. The flags were golden-colored . . .

The most significant love scene of this poem, the first meeting of Anirut and Usha, reads as follows:

The Literature of the Ayutthaya Period, 1350–1767

(328) When both awoke they thought to themselves: 'Maybe the spirit of the holy Sai tree with its widely spreading branches has united us.'

(329) Awake from sleep, both were greatly delighted, full of joy, and happy in the highest degree.

(330) 'Maybe we have achieved our dearest wish due to the merit acquired by both of us.'

(331) Both were happily united in a palace resplendent with crystal and a couch glittering with precious stones.

(332) They looked at each other. The king caressed the prodigious maiden. At their dramatic peak the verses run thus:

(335) Both beheld the other's beauty. They enjoyed it thoroughly. They hugged and caressed each other in close embrace as if fixed together.

(336) Both cast glances at each other stealthily, then looked away, and once again gave each other furtive looks. They snuggled up to each other in consuming desire. They enjoyed the bliss of love play and the highest rapture.

(337) Both were delighted and happy. Both lovers of royal blood enjoyed love making. They felt the prick of lust. (At Usha's) breasts they were united. . .

The story continues in this strain for another twenty-one verses in which certain parts of the body, Usha's necklace, and their couch are described in detail.

The range of Thai literature is, of course, far greater than the subject just reviewed. It should, however, be made clear from the outset that the Thais love the visual world of appearances and that their lives primarily center around concrete outer experiences. According to the teachings of Buddha, thirst for knowledge and unremitting inquisitiveness are not conducive to the Middle Path or the path of salvation. Knowledge is gained through meditation rather than metaphysical speculation. According to Buddha's doctrine life essentially involves suffering. In such a world, external phenomena like euphonious verses, the interplay of rhythm and harmonious rhymes are created to elevate everyday life to the level of art.

The first Thai textbook about language and poetry has come down to us from Horathibodi, the court astrologer and father of Si Prat. It is assumed that Phra Narai commissioned this work, entitled *Cindamani*, to be written for political reasons, since, during his reign western missionaries in Thailand tried, as a matter of course, to learn the vernacular and *Cindamani* afforded a good basis for their study. Until the turn of the twentieth century, *Cindamani* remained the unrivaled treatise on poetry and was at the same time *the* textbook for the study of the Thai language.

Thawathosamat, a cycle of some 260 verses, is the description of a fictitious journey through the twelve months of the year. Presumably, it was also composed during Phra Narai's reign. It is not known who the author of this work was. Narrated in the first person the poet describes the landscape, particularly the vegetation, and the social events occurring each month. April, for instance, is the hottest month and the time for kite flying. The erratic flight of the kites, pleasing to look at, is an expression of the poet's own sorrow and longing for his far-away sweetheart. A good many of the excessively lyrical verses make amusing reading. But, the story tends to get tedious when every minute detail, such as the flight of the kites in April and the fluttering ribbons tied to the ploughs in August, is used to express pangs of love. However, the poem is of great significance for a study of the cultural history of Thailand, offering an insight into the pattern of the people's life three hundred years ago.

Thawathosamat, even more than Si Prat's *Khlong Kamsuon*, is considered to have served as a model for the *nirat* poems which blossomed during the Bangkok period. Both the motifs as well as the structure of all later *nirat* poems are already fully developed in it. Things outwardly perceptible, animals, plants and landscapes, are their point of reference. Their characteristics, their beauty and scents are described, it is true, but these descriptions serve as a backdrop for the poet to give expression to his own emotions which, in the *nirat*, is invariably a melancholic mood of yearning for love.

Three poems are ascribed to Si Mahosot: the *Khlong chaloem phra kiet Phra Narai maharat*, 'a Khlong poem praising King Narai,' the *Khlong nirat Nakhon Sawan*, 'an account of the journey to Nakhon Sawan', and the *Kap ho khlong* poem. As already mentioned elsewhere, the authorship of Si Mahosot is uncertain and cannot be proved anymore. It is, however, customary to associate his name with these titles.

The *Khlong* poem in praise of Phra Narai is one of the first examples of a literary genre that was to be recurrent in the following centuries, namely the eulogy. As a matter of course didactic poems such as *suphasit* or 'proverbs' are likely to emerge in Buddhist societies, whereas poems of the panegyric genre are likely to be produced in absolute monarchies. There is, however, no specific Thai terminology that corresponds to the eulogy or panegyric poetry evident in western poetics. In Thai the metres in which poems are composed give eulogies their

The Literature of the Ayutthaya Period, 1350–1767

name-in the present case it is khlong. Eulogies begin with an invocation to the ruler, (*the kham namatsakan*):

(1) Shiva, glittering three-fold eye   powerfully luminous!
    Great Lord, god, powerful   many-headed (Brahma)!
      celestial being
    Sitting enthroned   above the world
    Come and dispel our sadness   floating in the heavens
                                           above the earth

In this verse the king is equated to the Hindu trinity of Shiva, Brahma and Vishnu and is addressed as a god and powerful ruler of the earth. This does not, however, imply a deification of the sovereign. It is solely related to the gods of the Hindu pantheon who still play a certain role in Buddhism and the ceremonies of ancient Thailand. The poem goes on to describe a journey from the capital city of Ayutthaya to the north. The reason for the journey is given in verses (2), and (3).

(2) The majesty reverentially received   the message
    a white cow elephant of   greatest beauty has been seen.
    He is to set out in his vehicle   into the forest.
      glittering with gold
    May the white elephant be a   admired by everybody.
      blessing to the country.

Right up to recent days the discovery of a 'white' elephant was regularly recorded in the chronicles as a state event of the first magnitude. But there was also another reason for which the king undertook this journey to the north:

(3) The majesty sets out   with a great battle force
    in order to attack the   There will be fighting!
      city of Chieng Haen.
    The many Lao on this   annihilated in great numbers
      earth shall be reduced
    The Lao tremble before the   in every small and big principal-
      ity
      power of the majesty and
      are afraid

13

At this juncture it is worth digressing into the non-literary world. We read, 'A great number of Laotians must be annihilated'. Now, if we recall, the cradle of Thai culture stood in this northern region of Thailand and the poet writes about the inhabitants as if they were a swarm of insects to be exterminated and that 'the people tremble at the sight of the majesty'. In the seventh century the sense of solidarity was quite obviously not very strong among the Thai speaking people. At the time, they were evidently far away from the concept of national unity and cohesion. The Lao resisted the ruler of Ayutthaya's claim to power and hence was an enemy just like the Mon and the Burmese.

Of even greater poetic appeal than the two poems mentioned earlier is Si Mahosot's *Kap ho khlong*. *Kap ho khlong* is the designation of a metre and means *kap* (verses) envelop *khlong* (verses). The relationship between the two metres has been described aptly in a textbook on Thai poetics. Parallels are drawn between the *kap* verse and a nutshell and the *khlong* verse and a stem of bamboo or sugar cane. It is obviously with premeditation that the author of the work on Thai poetics has selected these comparisons to present unwieldy material in a nutshell. Although the comparison is perhaps slightly exaggerated it clearly shows the existing tension between the two metres. The *kap* verses play the leading part in that they contain the main motives without, however, degrading the *khlong* verses to a mere padding of secondary importance. Striking the right balance depends on the talent of the poet. The two metres are like intertwining strands, the first line of the *kap* verse, in most cases, recurs as the first line of the *khlong* verse, literally or nearly so, being at any rate consonant with its general meaning. In some cases the consequent *kap* lines are repeated in the corresponding *khlong* verse. It should also be mentioned that *kap ho khlong* poems are as a rule predominantly of an erotic nature.

The poems of Si Mahosot are couches in terms suggestive of rather cheerful moods. They depict the courtship of the young at nightfall or at nocturnal hours in the carefree atmosphere of ancient Thailand.

Kap ho khlong:

(2) O beautiful night, bright sky!
    Excited voices on the river bank.
    Couples closely embraced they stare at each other.
    One can see their teasing play and the beat of their hearts.

The Literature of the Ayutthaya Period, 1350–1767

O beautiful night, bright sky,   beauty revealed!
Shining light suddenly radiates   from heaven.
The great feast and the flirting   of the people.
Courtship came to an end
They turn their faces in orderly   sitting in a circle
   manner   looking around.

In verses (3), (4), and (8), the clothes, finery, and above all the beauty of women are described in detail. They have 'radiant faces, round hips, firm and shapely breasts and well-groomed hair,'. In verse (7), is mentioned, not without mockery, 'whose breasts are sagging' and who 'stoops forward to cause their breasts to protrude'. Others again wear 'hair toupees, are plump and stout', as related in verse (9), or 'dainty and shy'. There is a variety of tastes and every single one is praised. Everything is aptly depicted and lines are drawn with a sure hand. But the poet's supreme mastery is revealed especially in his description of precarious and strait circumstances of young people in courtship, their fussy behavior and propensity to display themselves. 'How they are strutting about as in heavenly fields', verse (1), how they 'gape at each other', how men 'stare at' the maidens.

(5)   They stroll into the centre all at the time
      and snap their fingers
      waving their clothes and whistling a song.
      The young men, the noisy beat of the drums,
      the melodies, o this excites the women.

      They stroll into the centre   whistling a song.
         all at the same time
         snapping the fingers,
      The handsome lovers stroll   all calling at the same time.
         making noises,
      The women listen uneasily in   in sweetness and voluptuousness
         expectation
      There is smiling. The bees are   Touching. Singing in chorus.
         attracted by the fragrance,   Looking eye to eye.

15

(6) Walking to and fro, swarming,—delightedly.
The women let their eyes roam, they hope . . .
but stealthily from behind.
The shadow-play does not please them, they turn away.
Men move to and fro like the wind   for pleasure.
Young women, their eyes meet   but they resist.
Stealthily and from afar   they turn around shyly,
outwardly they are proud, but   and excited by love.
their thought bent on
voluptuousness

(10) Gentle sweetness! Lovers hasten
Lost by love—for which they would fight to death.
Oppressive fragrance wafting, arousing the males.
They cannot repress the urge aware of it all the time, searching

Gentle sweetness!—Lovers hasten   everyone.
(Even) asleep, there is excitement   forever.
craving and longing
Oppressive fragrance comes on   hot and delightful
wafting arousing them
I would walk by your side forever   closely embracing your
tender body.

'Bees' attracted by the fragrance of blossoms are mentioned in verse (5). This is a literary metaphor which is recurrent in Thai literature. Bees represent the male element and flowers represent the female element which are drawn to one another through the medium of fragrance and color uniting in love's rapture.

The death of Phra Narai marks a turning point in political history. The consequent change of sovereigns resulted in bloody fighting among the factions. Law and order did not prevail until after Boromakot's accession to the throne in the year 1735. The king himself was a poet of no mean reputation and his residence thus once again became the cultural centre of the country.

In this golden phase of the history of the Ayutthaya period literary production was primarily associated with the name of **Cau Fa Thamathibet**, one of Boromakot's sons and his presumptive successor.

The Literature of the Ayutthaya Period, 1350-1767

The lyrical quality of his language has remained unrivaled and no literary history book or cultural treatise fails to eulogize him as one of the greatest Thai poets the beauty of whose verses is unsurpassed. Even today his poems are included in every school syllabus as required reading.

His life story offers ample material for a full-scale novel which would be, it appears, the only adequate tribute to this imaginative spirit. Cau Fa Thamathibet was born in presumably 1715 and died in 1755, clubbed to death by the executioner. Prior to this he was charged with attempting to murder a rival successor to the throne. Being pardoned he retired into a monastery and lived the life of a monk until his nomination as successor to the throne. His end was brought about by a love affair he had with two wives of his royal father, a crime that was sanctioned by the law with capital punishment. His most renowned verses, the literary genre of which has come to be regarded as almost synonymous with the poet's name, are contained in the 'boat-songs', *kap he rua*. It is assumed that these songs were originally composed to accompany the rhythm of the oarsmen at work. In ancient Thailand rowing boats were the chief means of transport. Presumably the songs also gained popularity through the veneration of animal, tree and water gods—a practice common at the time. This is indicated by the very titles of the songs, namely, 'boat songs in praise of birds, flowers, fish'.

The songs do not convey any profound metaphysical meaning. They merely offer an unreflected, simple description of nature, and an enumeration of animals and plants. They bear witness to the Thais' attraction to the superficial, a result of their cultural evolution. There is a definite reluctance to analyze phenomena, and an aversion to lift the subconscious to any level of intellectuality. Cau Fa Thamathibet, however, also encompasses other subjects in his poetry,: 'boat songs in praise of Kaki, of copulation, of nostalgia'. Erotica is not alien to Thai poetry. Yet, the degree to which he describes personal passion in these poems is not typical of the Thai character, and no other Thai poet has ever written so uninhibitedly.

The boat songs of Cau Fa Thamathibet abound with mythological allusions which tend to make reading rather difficult for some students. Many of the allusions and finer nuances evident in his work are likely to escape the notice of those unable to read Thai. For instance, in the second verse of the 'Boat Song in Praise of Flowers' Nang Yaem, a particular type of flower is mentioned. But, yaem also means 'to smile'. In this sense the word is resumed in the third line of the *kap* verse.

Thai Literature

Khlong

> With good speed the boat of men   in their variety
> moves along the magnificent display   of subtle fragrance.
>   of flowers
> The flower-cups are on the point of   reaching forward in tufts.
>   opening, in colorful arrangement
> Enticing scents are hanging in the   like the scent of my
>   air stimulating desire   sweetheart's body.

Kap

(1) With good speed the boat moves along the array of flowers
of countless species along the river bank.
The flower-cups are on the point of opening in colorful arrangement
spreading a subtle scent like that of my sweetheart

(2) I praise the abundance of Nang Yaem.
One can see the tender pollen of the cups.
I remember the time when a smile flashed
from your mouth which delighted me, dear beloved.

(3) Campa, blossom of blossoms,
unfolded, yellowish, radiant, shining.
I think of my sweetheart, my dear beloved
of her skin brighter than golden Campa.

(4) Prayong blossoms droop like garlands
in clusters like colorful ornaments,
like the flowers decorating your white
body; O, I do praise you.

(5) Phutcip petals gently unroll,
Phikun is mixed with Sukrom.
The wind carries their full fragrance hither.
It is like the scent of my sweetheart who is on my mind.

The Literature of the Ayutthaya Period, 1350–1767

Boat Song in Praise of Birds

Khlong

The sun has scarcely gone down   in the west,
fading he hides behind mount Meru night is falling.
He has gone down—my heart is   my beloved as one longs for
  longing for   a mother.
Dim (is the sky) I am waiting for her turning around in bewilderment.

Kap

(1) The sun is fading and slowly setting,
    he will be down in a moment.
    Dusk is drawing near.
    I am thinking of your countenance, so beautiful.

(2) Hardly perceptible, on good order,
    birds fly near and turn sideways, the whole flock.
    One of them, however, parts from his mates,
    to be alone as I am.

(3) I see peacocks fanning out their tails.
    I think of your gracious movements, my beloved.
    Bird 'Gold necklace' stealthily parts
    as you beloved rush along in dancing gait. . . .

A few explanatory remarks must be added here in regard to the three different versions of the 'Boat Song in Praise of Kaki'. According to the cultural tradition of the Thai speaking people, Kaki is the embodiment of a depraved woman given solely to the pleasures of the body. Although Cau Fa Thamathibet follows the tradition, the euphony of his harmonious verses transpose the stigma of Kaki to a higher level. The male partner of Kaki, referred to in verse (1) by the pronoun 'he' and the 'bird' mentioned in verse (6) are the mythological Garuda or the Thai 'khrut'. It is explicitly clear that the 'nature' allegories described in verse (9) refer to sexual intercourse. Here the poet employs well known metaphors from Chinese lyrics.

Thai Literature

Boat Song in Praise of Kaki (*Khong doem*)

Khlong

He spreads his wings, holding you in embrace	Kaki.
His wings are flapping, he leads you beloved	to the silver cotton tree
A snake drooping from his beak is hurriedly carried away	it is a delicacy tree
Its tail strangles and throttles	everything has been prepared in the nest

Kap

(1) He spreads his wings, holds you in an embrace,
a beautiful, perfect figure.
His wings cover your breasts, slender woman
he touches and caresses them all over.

(2) A snake drooping from his beak is swiftly carried away,
it is a delicacy, its power of resistance already broken.
Its tail strangles him, writhing and wriggling.
However, we descend through the clouds towards the silver cotton tree.

(3) In my love nest in the golden palace
I am happy, beautiful Kaki, enjoying your embrace.
Vehemently I thrust into you again and again
You arouse my desire.

(4) In high spirits I caress your cheeks,
feeling the form of your breasts, you beautiful flower
take your body in my arms, beautiful one,
then, irrefutably, I lie with you in the lust of flesh.

(5) Kaki, you slender, delicate woman!
Devoutly you salute me,

and bend your head imploring me,
sadly concealing your face, staring to the ground.

(6) A bird jubilant with great joy,
is happy, happy, happy!
In utter harmony we embraced each other
joyfully responding to the play of love.

(7) Two are happy in lustful copulation.
Two strive to be one in an embrace of supreme rapture,
Two are drawing closer in a tight embrace, united,
Two are like one.

(8) How charming is your face, smiling
when we are together as we wish to be.
Blushing with the exertion of love and lust
you are even more beautiful than before.

(9) Wind blows strongly, parts the clouds
the heavens thunder, there is lightning with dazzling flashes.
Rain pours down incessantly
The waters of the ocean flow into your womb.

(10) A sea-dragon, delighted and in ecstasy
full of lusty excitement swims through the waves.
Two pressing close to each other.
Our pleasure will last forever.

Boat Song in Praise of Kaki (*bot khong doem*)

Khlong

With her hands Kaki fends off   the wings of Garuda.
Why do you come to hold me by force and embrace me?
Do you not fear my king   and consort?
You dare utter flattering words tempting and deceptive.

Thai Literature

Kap

(1) Kaki fends off with her hands
she cannot help touching (the bird's) wings.
This causes her excitement, blushing, and temptation.
Boundless is her heart's confusion.

(2) Kaki responds with suave words
arrogant are your deeds!
Fear you not the king
the perils attendant upon your rash actions?

(3) Though you are familiar with leisurely play,
I am not so inclined; desist from your plans.
Surely you are lord
and master of divine descent.

(4) You lead a heavenly life in a golden palace
with all the wonders at your feet.
You should not come trying to pay court (to me)
if we unite, hell is our destiny.

(5) For all you said to lead me to pleasure
to supreme happiness and joy,
for all your eloquent words I thank you,
but it cannot be, stop speaking!

(6) Khrut listens to the most beautiful woman
and caresses the tender one.
You heavenly flower on par with Montha,
your words are rash, equally angry and lovely.

(7) I dare be careless and bold
no one can help loving a beauty like you
as one loves heaven and earth.
I fear not the consequences, I am full of longing.

(8) Pray, trust in my devotion and my heart
to the end of life.
Having said this, he seized her in his arms
and kissed the beautiful one.

'The Boat Song in Praise of Kaki' is directly connected with the 'Boat Song in Praise of Copulation'—which is absolutely unique in Thai literature. It is a beautiful, tender, passionate, and sentimental poem all at once—equally remote from pornography or lewd ecstatic rapture. Similar in content and mood are the 'Boat Songs in Praise of Nostalgia'.

Boat Songs in Praise of Nostalgia (II)

Khlong

> This cheerful laughing voice whose is it?
> Is it the voice of my beloved I want to know.
> or of someone else?
> This cheerful youthful voice of my beloved. Come!
> Of course the voice is yours it cannot be someone else's.

Kap

(1) This cheerful laughing voice!
Is it my sweetheart's voice or someone else's?
This cheerful youthful voice
of my beloved, it follows me.

(2) The wind conveys my sweetheart's scent.
Fragrance enters my nostrils.
I am dreaming, see you approaching
I turn around, but a void prevails.

(3) It is midnight, the gong is struck.
Every night I beat my breast.
Wailing is the flute's sound,
I also wail incessantly.

(4) Three watches have passed.
The cock's cry is already barely audible
I was overcome by confused slumber and in a dreamy vision
you appeared before my eyes.

(5) Late morning—I have not had the pleasure to lie with you yet.
Infinite my sorrow and endless my longing
Overwhelmed by worry I weep
tears flow over my face.

(6) I was overcome by a hostile fate
of staying far away from you, lotus-like.
it is cruel and hard to bear.
Thinking of you I feel sad.

(7) You are beautiful, delicate, like a perfect picture.
Beautiful and charming are the movements of your hands.
You are beautiful indeed, smiling with restraint,
beautiful in uttering eloquent words expressive of excitement and desire.

(8) From morning to night
I bear my misfortune, am almost inured to it.
No one in this country.
is as sad as I am.

In addition to the twelve *kap he rua* poems, two of Cau Fa Thamathibet's *nirat* poems have been handed down to us: *Nirat kap ho khlong than sok*, and *Kap ho khlong than thong daeng*. Mention must also be made of two further works of purely Buddhist inspiration, namely, *Phra Malai kham luong*, and *Nanthopanantha kham luong*. Of these two *Phra Malai kham luong* gained fame in the course of time. It is the story of Holy Phra Malai who descends into the hells of suffering sinners and delivers them from their tortures as long as they listen to his sermons. This subject has been dealt with many times in Thai painting and sculpture.

The *Bunnowat kham chan*, which is assigned to the monk **Mahanak**, dates back to the reign of Boromakot. It contains the legend of the origin of the footprint of Lord Buddha near Saraburi, located about fifty-five miles north of Bangkok.

The Literature of the Ayutthaya Period, 1350–1767

The major part of the poem does not go beyond describing the royal pilgrimage to the sanctuary. This description contains some valuable information of interest for the cultural historian. Its poetic value, however, is of minor significance.

Example, 125 pp.
The repast was taken in a jovial mood. The party then roamed the woods conversing in a friendly manner. When at nightfall the sun set behind mount Meru, the birds screeching loudly made for their nests in the woods.

Example, 150 pp.
An army (of foot soldiers) was raised, equipped, with shields, lances and bows, with sabers, square and round shields, with poisoned arrows and fire arms, innumerable in their abundance. . . .

Example, 240 pp.
Sweet scent spread along the roads. The ladies
in attendance were enchanted by it.
As if his mind had changed suddenly, the king
turned to admire the birds. . . .

The beginning of the eighteenth century gave rise to a new literary form, the so called theatrical poetry called *lakhon*, so named because the term theatre does not assume the accepted western connotation. No dynamic or excessively intense dialogue is presented to the audience. Instead, players positioned in the front of the stage, recite texts of an epic nature which are mimed with dumb gestures. It is only at intervals that the players engage in brief dialogues.

There are two distinct types of *bot lakhon*: the *bot lakhon nai*, and the *bot lakhon nok*. The 'interior' lakhon or court lakhon was performed exclusively within the precincts of the royal court; the 'exterior' lakhon was designated for commoners. The former was rigidly stylized to suit the refined taste of court circles, the latter was rough and ready with a faster moving and more liberal sequence of movements. The *lakhon nai* was performed only by women, the *lakhon nok* only by men. The subjects of the plays were taken from the three major epics: the *Ramakien* which is a Thai version of the Indian *Ramayana*; the *Inau* of Javanese origin, and the *Unarut*, a version of the *Anirut* tales. Texts used in the *lakhon* nai performances were not permitted in the *lakhon nok*. These rules prevailed without exception until the reign of Rama IV, King Mongkut, 1851–1868.

Two of Boromakot's daughters are said to have individually composed a *bot lakhon* which have not, however, been preserved.

The historic Ayutthaya period came to an end in the year 1767. As a result of the devastation of the capital city of Ayutthaya a great number, perhaps the major part, of the manuscripts preserved there were destroyed. Owing to this unfortunate turn of events what has come down to us of early Thai literature is only fragmentary.

The Thonburi Period, 1764–1782

The Thonburi period—which derives its name from the (new) capital city—was a phase of national reconstitution during which public affairs were dominated by current military campaigns. Given these conditions, no room was left for cultivating literature and the fine arts. It is, however, known that in 1770 King Taksin was preoccupied with several sections of the *Ramakien* transforming them into *lakhon* stage plays. It should be noted, however, that they have never been performed since they were found unsuitable for adaptation to pantomime and dance.

What we also owe to the Thonburi period is **Cau Phraya Khlang**'s contribution. He headed the Ministry of Finance with the title 'Phra Khlang' during the reigns of Taksin and Rama I.

Inau, a *bot lakhon* set in chan metre, contains an episode from the wide range of the epic *Inau*. The poem *Phet Mongkut* which in Thai means 'jeweled crown' is based on a tale from the Indian cycle of fairy tales *Pancatantra*. It is a kind of court poetry obviously composed during hours of leisure to while away the time.

The Bangkok Period, 1782–1932

The year 1782 beckoned a new period of Thai history. This new dynasty turned back the hands of time to the year 1767 and seemingly continued the literary pursuits of the Ayutthaya period.

Literary production seems to have evolved over time, yet one can not accertain the extent to which scholarly works were destroyed forever during the last days of the old capital.

Rama I, who reigned during the years 1788–1809, is portrayed in chronicles as a statesman, politician and soldier all at once. It was, however, common for Thai kings to have a literary inclination, an attribute which contributed to their good reputation. The degree to which Rama I actually cooperated in composing the verses that have been handed down to us can only be left to conjecture.

The least significant work of Rama I to judge from a literary point of view, is *Phleng yau nirat rop phama thi tha din daeng*. This is a *phleng yau* poem describing the journey to Tha Din Daeng undertaken in order to defeat the Burmese. An account is given of the deployment of the Thai army at Tha Din Daeng near the Three Pagodas Pass where a decisive victory was won over superior Burmese forces in 1786. The poem keeps within the traditional bounds of eulogistic combat reports containing no new aspects of strategic relevance. The verses however set out in relief what is only sketchily touched upon in nondescript words in the chronicles. War at that time was not such a terrible thing in so far as the actual fighting was concerned. Apparently, it was a pleasant thing to look at one's own pennants flying and to see the enemy forces retreating—no one being really intent upon their utter physical destruction.

The Bangkok Period, 1782–1932

Example, 317pp.

The main force of the Burmese army is in hasty retreat.
Some die, prostrate on the ground.
By strength of the virtue once acquired
(we shall) receive help through providence.
We praise the Buddha's teachings.

The significance of the *Phleng yau nirat rop phama thi tha din daeng* is peripheral to Thai literature. Yet, it is of interest to us as an historic document and is perhaps the only remaining personal testimony of Rama I, founder of the Cakri dynasty.

Apart from this, Rama I composed some *lakhon* stage plays the subjects of which were borrowed from the epics already mentioned and from the *Anirut kham chan*. It also appears that the king was involved in revising and editing the text of the *Ramakien*, the most comprehensive Thai epic whose textual history is, to a large extent, yet unexplored. But it is almost certain that the epic has received its present form under the first two Cakri rulers Rama I and Rama II.

The poet most renowned during the reign of Rama I was **Phra Khlang** (about 1750–1805). He opened new vistas in the literary scene of his country not so much by his own creations but through his great translations of works from neighboring cultures.

'The Three Realms' or *Sam kok*, a translation of the Chinese historic novel *San-kuo-Chi T'ung-su Yen-i* set in the Han-period (168–265), achieved wide circulation. The translation is rather long-winded and too close to the original wording in many places. Nevertheless, it is easy to understand since foreign words are almost completely avoided. The work dates back to the year 1802 which is probably when the translation was completed. In its present-day printed form the Thai text comprises some 1500 pages in folio.

The second work translated into Thai by Phra Khlang, or, which in part he had had translated for him, is the historic novel *Ratchathirat*, or 'The King of Kings'. The novel contains an event from the history of the Mon based on a chronicle from Pegu (Burma). It is said that Rama I personally ordered the translation with a view to give literary expression to his endeavors to subject the southern Mon states of Burma to his rule and to foster a rapprochement of the Mon and the Thai people. The translation of the *Ratchathirat* makes easy reading. Both works *Sam*

Thai Literature

kok and *Ratchathirat* mark the time when the Thais were first acquainted with non-technical prose writing. This, however, was no incentive for the Thais to take to literary prose writing. For almost another hundred years Thai literary production strictly remained within the framework of versified poetry.

Phra Khlang published some more poems of various content and metres, among which were *Phet Phuong Mahachat* and a *khlong* poem entitled *Kaki*, based on a Jataka tale (No 327 or 360). This is his most charming versified narration. Kaki who has already been mentioned in connection with Cau Fa Thamathibet, is the wife of King Phromatat of Benares. The latter was one day visited by a Garuda (Khrut), a mythological being, half bird and half man, which the god Indra uses for riding. The Garuda plays chess with the king. While they are playing the beautiful Kaki appears and the Garuda falls in love with her. On the eve of the same day he abducts her and flies with her to his realm. After Phromatat notices her disappearance he consults with his servant Khonthan who immediately suspects Kaki has been abducted. Seven days later the Garuda returns to Benares to be received by Phromatat with his usual civility. As always they played a game of chess together. When the Garuda was about to return to his own realm, Khonthan transformed himself into a flea hiding under one of the bird's wings. He then encounters Kaki in the Garuda's palace and makes a declaration of love to her. Kaki accepts his courtship and both surrender to making love in the absence of the Garuda. Seven days later, the unsuspecting Garuda takes Khonthan back to Benares as a flea. During a renewed game of chess between Phromatat and the Garuda, Khonthan begins to sing a song mocking the Garuda. He, Khonthan, had been to the Garuda's palace and had made love to Kaki for seven days. Full of shame and wrath the Garuda leaves and repudiates Kaki: 'Your heart resembles water./ Indiscriminately it flows into brooks and lakes/ anywhere possible./ I am sorry for your beauty./ Your heart is so vile like an over-ripe fig/ outwardly shining red like a lotus blossom/ yet inside full of worms eating the flesh./ Now I know your heart/ yet in this night I will take you back to your own city.'

Two more poets who lived in the reign of Rama I are deserving of being mentioned. They did not produce any outstanding work but are, nevertheless, typical of the period. The king's bother **Mahasurasinghanat** who, as a military commander, played a prominent role in the wars against Burma. In his *Nirat Nakhon Si Thamarat* and the *Nirat ti Phama* he described two military campaigns. Both of these works may be attributed an analysis similar to the one offered for the king's *Nirat Tha Din Daeng*.

The Bangkok Period, 1782–1932

Thama Pricha, a courtier in the reign of Taksin (c., 1750–1810) was commissioned by Rama I to write a version of *Traiphum Phra Ruong* which should be easy to understand. It was published under the title *Traiphum Phra Ruong Lok Winichit*—an essay about the worlds.

Rama I, reorganizer and military leader, was succeeded by his son Phra Phuthaloetla who reigned as Rama II from 1809 until 1824. When he succeeded to the throne Thailand was a country well administered at home, maintaining balanced external relations. Under these conditions the king's residence became again a centre of the fine arts. Rama II was probably the most artistically inclined ruler of the Cakri dynasty. **Prince Damrong**, the great Thai historian, once observed that those with military merits were favored by Rama I whereas Rama II was partial to outstanding poets.

The reign of Rama II with its influence on literary circles which was noticeable even in the era of Rama III may well be considered as the most significant and productive epoch of Thai literature. The literary forms and contents of the time are to a considerable extent representative of the high standing of the literary production of the Thai people. As a standard they remained valid beyond the turn of the present century right into modern times. A study of Thai culture without considering the literary production of the nineteenth century would at best be fragmentary.

A considerable number of *lakhon* stage plays was produced, partly by the king himself. His most popular works are *bot lakhon Ramakien* and *bot lakhon Inau*. Both are considered classic pieces of their genre owing to their transparent structure which is particularly well suited to the requirements of the stage. Apart from poems based on the great traditional narratives Rama II also composed some *bot lakhon* the content of which is based on folk literature such as *Kraithong*, *Chaiyachet*, and *Khawi* and is in line with the tastes of the common man. Their contents have already been described above in connection with the first Thai versified poems. These poems are a gold mine for religious and cultural historians because of the animistic allusions they contain. For the literary historian, however, it is sufficient to read only one of them. As a further characteristic of this kind of literature and, implicitly, of the fundamental moral attitude of the respective poets, it should be noted at this juncture that the Thais' outlook towards moral failure or misdemeanor and death attendant upon it, differs fundamentally from that of westerners. To take passionate revenge would go against the natural disposition of the Thai character. The Thais would not have dragged Hector around the walls of Troy! At the moment of death all living beings are subjected to the Law of Suffering and the never ending cycle of rebirth—a fact which deserves man's compassion rather than condemnation or hatred. In consonance with this doctrine even the cruelest demon in fairy tales or narratives is accorded the same compassion, and departs this world in the same dignified way, as the mightiest and noblest king. Another observation important for literary sociologists is that in the overwhelming majority of cases the protagonists in the plays are princes of royal blood. Only in exceptional cases does a hero emerge from the common people as is the case in Kraithong.

With a view to introducing the reader to the fantastic, nay abstruse, nature of these fairy tale accounts is a summary of *bot lakhon nok Kraithong*:

A huge vicious crocodile once lived in an underwater cave near the town of Pichit in northern Thailand. All crocodiles took human shape in this cave. People were often scared by the giant crocodile. Nobody, however, was able to kill it because of its tremendous strength. Once a rich man made it known that he would give his two daughters in marriage to whoever would kill the mighty crocodile. Kraithong, a crocodile hunter well-known in his day also heard of this. He dived into the beast's cave and succeeded in killing it. At the same time, however, he fell in love with the crocodile's wife, who was known to be a beauty. Back in the human world Kraithong was married off to both daughters of the rich man. Moved by his longing for the wife of the slain beast left behind in the cave, Kraithong once again dived down and took her with him as his wife. Living with one wife in peace and harmony may be difficult, but living with three at the same time defies all chances of peace and harmony. It is the perpetual squabbles, intrigues and scenes of jealousy that have made this particular *lakhon* attractive to listeners and readers right up to the present day.

It was also during the reign of Rama II that **Sunthon Phu** began his literary work—one of the greatest poets according to our present day judgment of Thai literature. The statue erected in his memory near Klaeng has become a national sanctuary. His name is in every school-book or anthology.

Sunthon Phu lived from 1786 until 1855. From one of Prince Damrong's essays (available also in a French translation) we have an outline of the poet's biography; however, it contains many uncertain points. Sunthon Phu spent at least part of his life on his own as a Bohemian and it is presumed that on several occasions he had conflicts with his princely patrons, a fact which caused his imprisonment and financial hardships. The poet frequently complains about the latter in his verses.

The Bangkok Period, 1782–1932

The important place Sunthon Phu occupies in Thai literary studies compels us to question what his special literary qualities were—qualities that justified this high rank. The fame of his literary production could not possibly have lasted for more than 150 years if it were merely based on special circumstances of life or a complex personality.

What is the role he really played in Thai literary history? This is a two-sided question: the part he objectively played through the quality of his verses judged by the rules of literary criticism, and the part that was granted him by his contemporaries and by the present-day literary world. Was Sunthon Phu the culminating point of a literary tradition extending over three to four hundred years, or was he the starting point of a literature of the future? The review of Thai literature is by no means complete yet. The questions raised above are important and weighty ones but can at present be answered only tentatively in a very dithering or hypothetical manner.

Even though our knowledge about Thai literature anterior to the beginning of the Bangkok period is uncertain and incomplete there can scarcely be any doubt that all of the literary genres Sunthon Phu made use of were known and used long before him. This goes for the *nirat*, the *suphasit* and for the *bot lakhon* as well. Hence, Sunthon Phu followed in the footsteps of previous poets and the outer framework he found without adding a new literary genre. It should be mentioned that it was probably under his decisive influence that the structure of the *bot lakhon* was developed and expanded to assume the dimensions of a major epic, for it would be anachronistic to describe *Phra Aphaimani*, *Inau* and *Khun Chang Khun Phaen* as a mere *bot lakhon*. These poems, by virtue of their sheer volume, are no longer texts to be recited on the stage and accompanied with music and song for the amusement or edification of the audience, but they are epics designed with a great attention to detail and attain, in some parts, the level of world literature.

Besides form, metrics is also part of poetry and in this respect we should note Sunthon Phu's repeated reference to himself as *nak klon* and *nak leng klon*, cf., *Ramphan philap* (392). There were poems written in this metre before Sunthon Phu, it is true, but it was he who turned this metre into its present state, a metre in which the euphony and rhythm of the Thai language develop in the most beautiful manner. This, in fact, is the most essential contribution Sunthon Phu made to the formal development of Thai poetry which was more than merely a new scansion or a new rhyming pattern. Scarcely noticed by his contemporaries the poet thus gave expression to a slowly developing self-awareness of the Thai people. It was the autochthonous element, freed from alien examples, that won the upper hand in the nation under the guidance of its poetry.

The fact that the poet freely mentions his posts, activities, or habits points to the considerable polar tensions from which he strove to free and, at the same time, to sublimate himself. He describes himself emphatically as *samien*, royal scribe; as *nak klon*, poet of klong; as *alak*, secretary; as *khru* teacher; as *kawi*, poet; as *nak buot*, monk; as *mahatlek*, page or courtier;—but also as *khon khuk*, prisoner; *pho kha*, trader; and as *khon dit lau*, an addict to alcohol. The dignity and reputation of an *alak* as a rule precludes any comparison with a *khon khuk*, and there is no bridge between a *nak buot* and a *khon dit lau*. We can assume that at the beginning of Sunthon Phu's career as a poet the Thai language was already fully developed—apart from idiomatics, a field which even today is subject to constant changes. Hence, there was no hindrance for the poet to shape his verses with an ease that is *per se* pleasant sounding and harmonious even if the content of the verses remained insignificant. There are many possibilities in the Thai language to keep the precise meaning of a phrase in the balance. Since even today ideas can be expressed in rather vague and non-committal ways, the intellect of the Thais' was never challenged to extreme lengths. But just this, it appears, is a precondition for poetic talent to blossom in lively souls, a talent that is ultimately linked with an inability or unwillingness to interpret everything intellectually. It is true for many of Sunthon Phu's verses—as well as those of other poets—that the idea does not give birth to the word, but that the word generates the idea. Ideas are quite often the outcome of linguistic and literary inspirations of the moment, but in many instances also the outcome of instinctive routine. Writing poetry was for Sunthon Phu, *inter alia*, an act of personal liberation and artistic play.

Considering the great emphasis attached to form in Thai poetry the above mentioned is of much significance. The decisive message expressed by Suthon Phu in his verses has given an impetus and direction to the evolution of Thai poetry. A new style which could not have escaped the attention of his contemporaries evolved. Thai literature gained a new mode of poetic expression and displayed new contents and dimensions that were hitherto unknown. However, the reader was not warned by the beat of drums of what was in the offing. No manifesto announcing what was new was published. It just happened, without a period of transition, in so gentle a manner that is possible only within the Thai cultural environment. The time was not ripe then for a cultural or political upheaval. Still, just as the Cakri kings faintly realized the advent of an era with a

The Bangkok Period, 1782–1932

western stamp—a machine gun and gunboat era—and equipped themselves with a well organized central government and Buddhist church, the highly sensitive and gifted poet Sunthon Phu also gave expression in his verses to the subliminal currents he sensed in his social milieu.

With a view to further elucidate what has been said above, a comparison is drawn with the content and style of *klon nirat* poems written before his time. It is with some hesitation that we dare to refer to the *Phleng yau nirat phima thi din daeng* of Rama I or to the nirat of Uparat Surasinghanat. Did any other works of the *klon nirat* genre exist in Thailand prior to *Nirat Klaeng*? Certainly there were less known *nirat* before, the texts of which have not yet been printed and which literary historians were unaware of. These texts may be invaluable, but it is undisputed that the *klon nirat* first achieved fame on the literary stage through the works of Sunthon Phu.

No text, even remotely comparable to *Kamnoet Phlai Ngam*—a piece on par with world literature—was ever known in Thai literature before the time of Sunthon Phu. Setting aside for the present its high stylistic and aesthetic level, it is the undistorted, almost photographic way of depicting things, typical of this section of the voluminous epic *Khun Chang Khun Phaen*, which fascinates the reader. Furthermore, what is true of this masterpiece also applies to the other poems of Sunthon Phu. All are rooted in an objective world and real life. The reader can discover in them a portrait of the poet as well as his own portrait and that of his fellow beings.

Sunthon Phu's deviation from traditional themes is rather radical. Scenes depicting reality are also visible in the works of other poets such as Si Mahosot, however, viewed holistically their relationship to the poem is different. In the poems of the latter, the depiction of reality does not go beyond an expedient in the direction of the plot which inevitably centers around nothing other that the glorification of His Majesty. By way of contrast, Sunthon Phu's poems are not merely eulogies rooted in the world of fairy tales and fantasy. His *nirat* poems definitely do not belong to the genre of versified *nithan* or *niyai* (fairy tales, narrations). Despite this, the reader must still have to tolerate certain traditional aspects they contain, such as tedious accounts of things actually seen or imagined.

Sunthon Phu had the courage to behold and express things as they appeared—with certain reservations; he also had the courage to describe personal feelings beyond outdated stereotyped patterns. He is one of the few Thai poets who reported and acted at the same time.

The plot structure of his *nirat* poems is invariably based on a journey to places from which the nirat poems derive their names. The itineraries can be checked even today, for most of the places visited still exist. Their inhabitants are by no means celestial but solid human beings whose characteristic traits are lovingly described in detail in some passages or censored by critical comments in others.

Criticism predetermines a certain measure of rational thought in the person that criticizes. In fact, Sunthon Phu's poems rarely deviate into the realm of fantasy or the region beyond the control of the intellect. There is no scope in his poems for powerful magicians, horses with giant strides or winged beings who can travel half the world with one step or a single flap of the wings. Rational thought is also promoted in intelligent men through Buddhism. If stretched too far, however, it may result in man's inability to perceive or appreciate magical phenomena altogether. Sunthon Phu expresses his views on this matter in a moderate way in his *Nirat Phra Pathom* (428 pp.).

To Sunthon Phu a journey was not just a past-time. It is true that journeys have destinations, but better than just arriving at a place for him was the process of familiarizing himself with things along the way—things that he could afterwards teach other people. He took notes of what he perceived and observed of strange and alien occurrences—be they the usefulness of certain plants or the peculiar geological formation of a river bank. Fortunately, his descriptions of localities do not possess the quality of topographical surveys, nor are his accounts about the flora and fauna of a place so precise as to taint the beauty of his poetry. There is enough left to the imagination of the reader.

Sunthon Phu conceives of the world as pure nature. This implies that his view of the world, at least the objective world, is the result of his personal experiences. There is no screen of any kind interposed between himself and nature; his view is unrefracted and free from doubts. This implies that time, in his mind's eye, is perceived in seasons and does not move in a linear historical procession but is cyclical with recurrent periods. Human life and the life of the soul are part and parcel of this cyclic movement and hence ever recurring. Nature, on the one hand is immense, profuse and perfect in itself —oceans, mountains and jungles—and on the other it is sparing in the use of its forces. Contemplating the overwhelming magnificence of nature may stifle the poet's creativity since he finds no resonance of the anguish of his tormented soul here. It is this very anguish that causes the unrest from which springs the poet's creativity.

One may question whether he merely describes the landscape as he actually sees it or whether his descriptions reflect his own perceptions. When, for instance,

The Bangkok Period, 1782–1932

the name of a woman springs to his mind he usually looks for a tree or shrub on the river bank bearing the same name which he associates with the woman on his mind. There is an expedient to express his feelings about her. The question is how often is the outside world a reflection of an inner vision and how often does a true description of nature give way to conceptions of the mind arising in the poet's soul. It is only on a few occasions that Sunthon Phu expresses his feelings about the beauty of nature without any reference to his personal suffering or yearning. The monotonous enumeration of trees, shrubs or flowers wouldn't be half as boring if written in a more rhapsodic or pathetic style. However, he who has gone through the ups and downs of life and gained an insight into the depths of the soul, prefers pondering on the surface of things by adopting trite expressions and clichés. At this juncture we will digress from not only the poetry of Sunthon Phu but from Thai poetry in general.

Why are trees, both big and small, in bloom or otherwise, mentioned repeatedly and occasionally described in detail? We know that the Thai mind, as it appears in literature, is molded to a considerable extent by relics of animism—a fact only admitted by most Thais with much reluctance. It is worthy to mention that trees have long been considered objects of great symbolism the world over.

Traveling by boat, the poet describes in one of his *nirat* poems what he sees. The mere mention of the names of the trees he encounters conjures up their scent in the poet's mind. Some of these scents are said to possess the specific effect of evoking sadness or joy. The effective aromatic substances of the plants, known as pheromones, have been discovered by scientific research. Verses of this kind can be found in many of the *nirat* poems. In the *Nirat Inau* for instance, 'the spirit of the Banyan tree is murmuring' (verse 322), in the *Nirat Nen Klan* 'a tree goddess is uttering murmurs' (627) with the effect that the boat of the travelers made further headway (636). Again and again the reader encounters discrepancies or the unison of a highly elevated intellect and an archaic awareness of life.

Sunthon Phu, the epitome of a sensitive race whose lifestyle was thoroughly determined by Theravada Buddhism, probably traced such verses back to *nithan chau ban*, i.e., tales of peasant people. But it might still be presumed that the constant enumeration of species of the native flora has its roots in the magical spheres of pre-Buddhist times. It is likely that the subconscious mind plays a significant part here. As has been said before, Sunthon Phu was more intent upon describing things as they appeared than freighting them with symbolism.

Knowledge and science being of existential importance to everybody, and especially to those wielding power, he does not cease to remind his readers in each of his poems of the advantages of specific knowledge in certain situations. This is no sign of an overbearing know-it-all attitude in him, but simply his personal endeavor to gain insights and to quench his thirst for knowledge. His keenness to gain insight has nothing to do with the bourgeoisie conception of education. The knowledge he strives for is not limited to what is necessary for physical survival but first and foremost comprises an insight into the fate humans are destined to. His mind centers around the concept of *kam*, in Pali *kamma*. In his works there are numerous references to *kam*. The significance of religion is uppermost in his mind. He conceives of religion as an instructive means to counterbalance the dangers to which the intellect is exposed by claims of the vital force. He is in no doubt that mankind is subject to the law of *kamma* just as he is in no doubt about the changing of the seasons. His awareness of his own transitory nature is predominant, so much so that there is no need for further intellectual efforts.

What knowledge is really necessary in order to cope with life?

(1) Knowledge of the essence of nature, especially in one's habitual environment.
(2) Knowledge of the customs and traditions of the country; awareness of one's place and part in society. The poet never fails to stress the latter in each of his poems.

And, there is yet another way to acquire knowledge, even for Sunthon Phu, the devout Buddhist who advocated rational thought. It is quite obvious from his writing that the elements of mysticism and magic have a strong bearing upon the Thai mind. His descriptions of *Phlai Ngam* (82 pp.) are of abstruse dimensions. Is it unreasonable for a person of Sunthon Phu's disposition (having suffered from recurring bouts of depression) to succumb to man's yearning for participation in the divine through magic? In the throes of depression he rebelled against strict logical reasoning involving the chain of cause and effect—and from which all supernatural powers are excluded and gifts of chance and luck denied.

The poet looks at the world from below, from the position of a *phrai*, i.e., 'a simple citizen.' His role is that of a direct observer whose view is not obstructed by any irrelevant concepts. It is this perspective that imparts the quality of a close relationship to everyday life and real things, including trivia, to his verses. His eyes are focused on things that are simple and typical, but that is not all. His perceptions give rise to a dialectical process of exchange between the outside world and his inner world. This dialectic sometimes points to a direction that is contrary to the trend in which a particular story or poem is directed. While the story of the *nirat* moves towards a given destination, Sunthon Phu directs his thoughts backwards. Names of flowers, for instance, bring back memories and associations of the past—this goes to show that man is basically a conservative creature who finds it difficult to adjust to changing situations and who has an inherent propensity to return to his original condition. In Sunthon Phu's writing this is given subtle expression by an asyndetic phrase or by comparison.

He describes his environment critically, at least as far as people are concerned. In character with his natural disposition he lays greater emphasis on being aloof rather than attached. He is full of unreserved praise, admiration, and approval in describing Buddhist edifices and sanctuaries, for example Nakhon Pathom Cedi in his *Nirat Phra Pathom*, the Phu Khau Thong in his *nirat* of the same name, and the Khau luong in his *Nirat Muang Phet*. The description of the Phu Khao Thong bears out that Sunthon Phu has fully grasped the conception of space present in Hindu-Buddhist cosmology. In his beautiful narration of Phu Khau Thong he states that the predominant vertical is an integral trait of Thai architecture (see *Nirat phu khao thong* 282 pp.). The three qualities that are inherent in traveling, as Claude Levi-Strauss writes in his *Sad Tropics* are also conspicuous in Sunthon Phu's *nirat*. 'Traveling is more than a mere change of place . . . a journey is made in space, in time, and in the social structures,' (chapter II)

All that has been written about Sunthon Phu must necessarily be of a fragmentary nature. In any case, it is an exciting venture to portray a strange person. Some features are likely to be depicted in glaring tones, others may be overlooked entirely, concealed, or distorted. Perhaps it's a blessing that we have only a scanty knowledge of Sunthon Phu's life, else we might discover some disconcerting truths. It is due to the indifference and negligence of his contemporaries and poets after his time that no precise evidence or documentation based on the life of this great writer has been handed down to us. Apart from *feuilletonistic* fabrications and apparently unmasking revelations it is highly unlikely that his biography can ever be attempted with the scanty resource material available. Sunthon Phu's work, however, will surely endure as one of the greatest milestones of Thai cultural history. His prolific imagination is outstanding; his often popular language secured for his writings wide circulation. Only on rare occasions does the poet use, in his works, words of foreign origin or an erudite vocabulary pertaining exclusively to higher learning. Although the idiomatic expressions and proverbial sayings used in his poems are not easy for westerners to comprehend they were readily understood by Thai readers in the early part of the nineteenth century.

For Sunthon Phu's kind of poetic expression it became necessary to develop a new metre. The *kham klon* had, in fact, been known since the end of the Ayutthaya

Thai Literature

period, however, it was introduced as a fully valid poetic medium and given its polished final shape by Sunthon Phu. The poet added to the exterior rhyme, linking the lines, a system of variable interior rhymes. In the Thai language, an interior rhyme is brought about by vocalic on consonantal assonance within a line, as shown in the following graph:
(Marks above the line point to consonantal, those below it to vocalic rhymes).

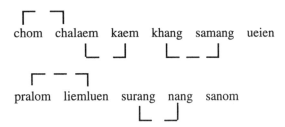

The interior rhymes in conjunction with the different tones of the syllables and the great variety of vowels in the Thai language go together to yield the softly lilting rhyme of the verses.

A substantial oeuvre has been handed down to us under the name of Sunthon Phu—the epic poem *Phra Aphaimani* alone comprises some 25,000 verses. Phra Aphaimani, the illustrious hero of the story, possesses magical powers which help him brave many dangers. The epic is not a mere account of external events. Sunthon Phu at times transcends the boundaries demarcating epic from lyrical diction. Much scope is given to the actors to express their emotions. The epic bears traces of having been published in series form since the poet quite obviously had to make a living from the sale of each installment. Transgressions and abrupt inclusions of new episodes may be likened to the novels of Dickens and Balzac.

Sunthon Phu also contributed to another epic poem, the most typical of all Thai epics, *Khun Chang Khun Phaen*. It is presumed that the content of the epic dates back to a story well-known in the Ayutthaya period. Its central theme is the rivalry between Khun Chang and Khun Phaen in their quest to win the beautiful Wan Thong. Khun Phaen is presented as a glorious hero hailing from poor conditions and rising to the level of an officer in the army of the king of Ayutthaya. He is courageous and handsome and familiar with magic and the courtship of women. His rival, Khun Chang, is the opposite in almost every respect, wealthy but uncouth, ugly, bald and plump. The character of the protagonists is still modeled on old patterns—a traditional scheme of the versified literature of the preceding centuries: a simple polarity of contrasting types. The poets of this epic, however, expand this old frame in a manner hitherto unknown. *Khun Chang Khun Phaen*, in the shape in which it is available to us today, is not only a high caliber poem but also a first-rate document of cultural history. Its evaluation and analysis has not yet even begun. It comprises mines of information invaluable for sociological research on ancient Thailand. From the point of view of literary history, even the metre in which the text was versified, namely, the *klon sepha* is of interest. *Sepha* designates a versified story, destined for recitation, with special emphasis on word tone and rhyme. Some parts of the poem had already been versified in the reign of Rama II.

According to Prince Damrong, it was Sunthon Phu who composed the famous 24th section of this *klon sepha* entitled, 'The Birth of Phlai Ngam.' However, this authorship can not be proved with absolute certainty—it is without question, however, judging by the mastery reflected in these 1116 verses, that they could only have been composed by a poet of great genius. The flexibility and beauty of the verses is equal to their formal precision. The poet does not revel in a flourish of fine words but consistently carries the action forth to its logical conclusion. He is not carried away by the pleasant sounds of words, but soberly depicts reality in a well defined way. Nothing is left to chance; his rhymes are not geared to preserve the fortuous deeds of others. The strict structure of the plot does not permit any digression or literary rank growth. Some of the passages have been heightened to dramatic dimensions in order to retain the reader's attention, while others have now become proverbial.

The heading of the 24th section of the epic, in its abridged form, falls short of epitomizing the whole content. It would be more appropriate to epitomize the story as follows: 'the birth of Phlai Ngam, the distress of his boyhood, and his maturing into adolescence.'

Khun Chang, Wan Thong's husband, finds out that he is not the real father of her son Phlai Ngam. Thereupon, he tries to kill the child with much cunning. With a view to preventing his murder Wan Thong resolves to take her son to his grandmother, the mother of his real father. The child takes leave of his mother thus:

Extract, 405 pp.

Phlai Ngam is full of compassion for his mother.
Looking at her he perceives tears running over her face

and kneels down before her in a loving gesture.
Once I am grown up I will come and look after you.
Destiny now decrees that we must part.
I must take leave of you because of this villainous man
and shall go in search of my father. Let me be lucky to find him
I shall not forget your kindness, mother, I shall come back.
Dear mother of mine, I know that you love me.
There is no one else like you, not in ten or a hundred thousand.
Whether eating or sleeping you will care for me.
When I leave you and your house, it is only my body that parts.
Wan Thong, mother of mine, now return to your house.
(Otherwise) the bad man will be angry with you, dear.
I shall depart with my head bowed, but not being afraid.
Do not worry, mother, pray take courage.

Wan Thong takes him in her embrace, kisses him and strokes his back,
    giving advice,
With tears in her eyes she gives her blessing to young Phlai Ngam.
Now proceed on your way with luck, protected from dangers —
Until you are grown up and have acquired merit as a monk.
The reputation of a youngster is borne out by his handwriting
Practice it with diligence!
Then she led the child to the place from where ox-carts start.
They will part here, with their hearts broken.
The child looks up at his mother, the mother down to her child.
They are so closely united to each other, as if blood flowed from their
    eyes.
Sighing and sobbing they take leave with their hearts throbbing.
The boy courageously parts from his mother and goes on his way.
He turns to look back and sees his mother looking after him.

Seeing the tender boy—she heaves a sigh.
But he looks aside, turns and disappears
Spreading before his eyes are fear and terror.

Wan Thong, moved by pain, fears Khun Chang,
He is not like other men. He is jealous.

> She turns and hurries along the edge of the fields.
> In a gloomy mood she enters the house.
> She weeps every night, every morning in dejection
> full of longing for her young boy Phlai Ngam,
> At meal time she has no appetite and eats but little
> becoming thin and her skin shriveling day and night.

The poem describes in terse and concise language Phlai Ngam's journey from Suphanburi to Ban Krang. Twice, it is true, allusions are made to his mental and emotional state, but for the rest the things he encounters on his way are mentioned without comment. He passes mountains, houses, and villages, 'walks right across the fields' and 'along ox-cart tracks.' The passages describing his childish pleasures are delightful reading. (458 pp.) In describing the vegetation the poet but once succumbs to the temptation to achieve a sonorous interior rhyme by means of accumulating plant names. 'Bunches of flowers are seen in abundance—as painted in a picture,' (450 pp.). This comparison is, in fact, a topos to be found in many Thai poems.

Extract, 445 pp.

> Phlai Ngam proceeds on his way across fields.
> Specially noting the mountains on his way. In a depressed mood he
>   forges his way forward.
> Proceeding past houses, the silhouette of palm trees standing in groups
>   in the flat country.
> Crammed together Takhien trees afford pleasant shade, fruit-bearing
>   Khae-khang-, krang- and krathum trees soar into the sky.
> Bunches of flowers in abundance—as in a picture.
> All this diverts Phlai Ngam's mind while proceeding on the cart tracks
> on the level ground a gentle breeze is blowing all the while.
> After passing the houses of the Karen, he arrives at a dwelling place
> with a gong, a pond and a bridge.
> He sees buildings, cotton wool plantations in the plain, right and left all
> pepper shrubs and aubergines, yellow gardens, beautiful to look at,
> Salika birds are picking on the ground and fly off.
> There are also chicken scratching the ground for bamboo seeds.
> With a shriek he sets them aflight and they make off in disarray.

Thai Literature

> He also comes across a large flock of peacocks who scurry away fanning out their tails.
> Scared they soar high and Phlai Ngam is pleased to see this.
> But he is tired, exhausted and begins to sway.
> He thinks of his mother, Wan Thong, and weeps.
> In the evening the sun is slowly setting, as
> His heart slowly breaks in two!
> At dusk he encounters a pack of small foxes
> busily sniffing around on the hills, barking and howling.
> He is frightened to the core and lapses into a yearning mood.
> He reaches the border of the wooded area around Kanchanaburi.
> There he sees a deserted temple on the slope of a hill. A very old temple indeed.
> It has only a single Buddha statue.
> Its old Ubosot windows and doors are still intact.
> Night is falling and he lies down to pass the night.
> At dawn he takes out his cake and fruits to eat to his heart's content, then heads for the mountains.
> He arrives at Ban Krang, meeting on his way people who carry heavy loads on their shoulders.

Verses (480–488) also make delightful reading. With childish unconcern grandmother Thong Prasi is described as a frightening hag whose maliciousness far exceeds that of demon Phi Sua Samut well-known from the *Ramakien*. Children never shy away from telling the truth: Thong Prasi is the *yai nom yau*, 'grandmother with the flabby breasts.' Phali Ngam asks playing children where his grandmother lives.

Extract, 480 pp.

> She lives over there in the fields that cannot be seen from here.
> A huge Mayom tree stands at the side of the house with very sweet fruit.
> Often we go there to steal some (however) she lies in wait to catch us.
> She once caught me and pinched me severely.
> She is malicious like Phi Sua, even worse.
> When a child goes there to play and she sees him approaching

The Bangkok Period, 1782–1932

she catches him, takes her breasts and beats the child's head with them.
Why do you come and ask for her? Are you not afraid?
She will catch you and beat you to death 'Grandmother- flabby- breasts.'

In the course of telling his story the poet, in verses 1057, directly points out the significance of the court ceremonial as a 'substructure' of the state machinery, indispensable for maintaining balance and stability. Through ceremonials the factual relationship between higher and lower levels of the hierarchy is shifted to a formal plane that does not permit the development of antagonistic patterns of behavior. This becomes clearly evident in verses 1071 pp. The rules of ceremonial and protocol kept large numbers of more or less ambitions courtiers busy and at bay diverting their thoughts from pondering intrigues or rebellions.

'It is exactly four o' clock, the king enters the palace.' The daily routine of the Thai kings was regulated by strict protocol. 'Royal duties', *ratchanukit*, were codified in minute detail in the palace law, the *kot monthienban*, (see verse 1028) among other places. The rhythm of the personal life of the majesty as well as that of governmental activities was determined by the palace law.

In contrast to what was hitherto usual in Thai poetry the poem devotes only little space to describing the power and splendor of the King and his court (verses 1077 to 1092). In measured, nay stilted, words Phra Muen presents Phlai Ngam to the King (verses 1095 to 1100) and is courageous enough to mention the name Khun Phaen, Phlai Ngam's real father whom the King had sentenced to a long term in jail.

'His august Majesty looks sideways and into Phlai Ngam's face with compassion. He is on the verge of opening his mouth to speak in favor of the suffering Khun Phaen, but at the same time inexorable fate causes his compassion to fade. Absent-minded, His Majesty contemplates other things' (verses 1101 to 1105). In fact, His mind was concentrated on a stage play! Verily, many as are the highlights in this poem, the verses quoted above are the crowning glory! The fortuitous character of history cannot be expressed in a more frightful, more banal and at the same time more human way. And it does not matter what is to be understood by 'inexorable fate', whether it is that of the King or, more probably, that of Khun Phaen. 'Nothing is uttered, (verse 1106) His Majesty forgets what ought to be said according to royal duty' (1107). All is banal to the highest degree. 'His Majesty proceeds to the royal bed-chambers,' It is hardly possible to describe in a more brilliant manner the true nature of history and its obvious lack of aim and meaning. And, what is more, the poet does not shrink from describing the 'august majesty' as a human being, not as 'godlike' and the 'seat of all virtues'. It is certain that the poet did not intend his verses to be constructed as a caricature. 'Inexorable fate', *kam*, is the central concept, at any rate, of the cultural community to which he belonged. It is not to be imagined as an idea brought forth by subjective inspiration. However, the way in which the poet gives expression to it is unique in the literature of the Thai. The assurance of his diction, the absence of all comment and doubt go to reveal the nature of the fated and inevitable. 'Nothing is uttered' is expressed in Thai by the plain everyday figure of speech *nuek mai ok*. Here we clearly see that there is no need for exalted words to give expressions to what is by any means inevitable.

Sunthon Phu's *nirat* poems, of which he has composed a fairly large number, are surely to be considered as the crowning of his literary work. Among others are, *Nirat muang Klaeng, Nirat Phra Pathom, Nirat Phu Khau Thong, Nirat Muang Phet, Nirat Wat Cau Fa*, and *Nirat Suphan*. This literary genre attains the highest peak of perfection through Sunthon Phu's contributions.

Essentially the *nirat* is a poem describing travel and leave taking. This implies movement and separation, i.e., restlessness and disquiet. A travel account deals with moving for a length of time to a certain destination, and returning again to the point of origin.

Traveling in Thailand in the old days was not a very comfortable affair, with the possible exception of employing royal means of transport on water or a roomy *howdah* on an elephant's back—without any need for caution along the way. Sunthon Phu's journeys were strenuous. He often complained about them deploring the wind and waves, mosquitoes, wild beasts, narrowness of the fairway and the resulting congestion, hunger and lack of accommodation. Notwithstanding these impediments, he sets out again and again for Phetburi—obviously more often than once—for Phu Khau Thong near Ayutthaya, for Nakhon Pathom, for Suphanburi, for Phra thaen dong rang, for Klaeng. Was he inspired by the joy of traveling or was it the sheer love of adventure? What else could have tempted him?

Surely it was his acute craving for knowledge, for gaining new experiences and perspectives, material for new poems. But, despite all these positive aspects a possible further motive must not be overlooked, namely fleeing from himself and others, his unrest and perhaps inner compulsion.

The author of this book is inclined to assume that for Sunthon Phu the desire to get away from it all, combined with a restlessness to be on the go, was the strongest motivation for composing the *nirat* poems. The flight from one place to

The Bangkok Period, 1782–1932

another; from the status of a layman to that of a monk, obviously each time in a different convent; his escape from women; his being drawn towards intoxicants such as alcohol; his fantasies and dreams (to which a whole elegy, *Ramphan philap*, is dedicated.) Every one of his *nirat* contains phrases such as 'If I had . . . I would do this,' etc. Such phrases should not be interpreted as an utterance of wishes through which the defects, imperfections or the lack of certain things are confessed. Such phrases, rather, are the projection of a deep-seated dissatisfaction or unfullfilment from which he strives to escape, an escape from the reality of the present. The present is at any moment subject to variations of consciousness and manned by imperfections and death. Hence, only the past and the future remain: either to revert thoughts back into a supposed paradise of the past or to project them into the future. The knight will periodically return to his narcissist paradise—to King Arthur's Court or the Holy Grail. Sunthon Phu's entire literary work may be regarded as offering the path to attain higher sublimation.

In the course of time some of his verses have been hyperbolized and come to be so-called 'Golden Words' often quoted by connoisseurs. The best-known of his verses are contained in passages (56) and (57) of *Nirat Phu Khau Thong*—passages which are, rightly or wrongly, of great relevance to his biography:

> Arriving at the distillery, heavy with smoke.
> A dipper with a handle is tied with a string to the end of a pole.
> O sinfulness, on evil fate, this hell-brave boils in my breast
> making me drunk like mad, it is a shame.
> Pray, let me succeed in making merit as a monk
> omniscient, enlightened Buddha, as it is my intent.
> From alcohol I could safely escape, it did not destroy me.
> It would be absurd not to go near it pretending to look away.
> Not alcohol alone makes us drunk, but love makes us drunk as well.
> Should thoughts of love also be repressed, I wonder?
> Drunkenness with alcohol, day or night, is passing
> but this heart drunken with love is drunken every night on end.

And here is another section of the same nirat (verses 240 pp.) which may well stand as a specimen of this poetic genre.

> In the harbor I pass by the house of the governor
> I remember bygone days and shed tears.

I would stop and pay a visit if he were still (old) Camuen Way.
He would be pleased to receive me in his residence.
But if he did—in predicament—he would do something unusual.
My heart would split in two, if he scolded me.
Can a man in misery hope for goodness? This should be avoided
I would lose face.
In the harbor I stop opposite Wat Phra Meru.
At the fringe of the temple boats ate moored in parallel rows,
Other boats glide by with cheerful singing.
Enticing songs ring out stimulating others.
Devout people offer robes to the monks and sing *sepha*.
Ranat xylophones project the songs—as (played) by Nai Seng.
Rows of lanterns shine brightly as in Sampheng.
At the moment, I am bent on myself, have no desires, but I am aware nevertheless.
In half the boats *klon* (verses) are sung with great relish
drawn out to such length as to offend the ear.
Yet no end of it, a tiring repetition like the wriggling of a snake.
The chorus repeats the songs—in a drowsy mood,
Other singing comes from the side of the temple.
Eventually there is stillness and I can fall asleep on the cushion,
About three o'clock in the morning a thief stealthily sneaks near, enters,
pilfers things and leaves the boat again,
The boat tips with a gurgling sound : I shout and
the villain deftly and swiftly dives into the water.
I do not even see the familiar pupil.
I am confused like a madman and excited
Nu Phat managed to light a candle
Nothing of the yellow outfit, the eight (monkish) utensils are missing.
The power of meditation and merit and heavenly grace
won a victory over all—as I had hoped for,
At dawn in the morning a festive day lay ahead,
I devoutly venerate the scared law
and proceed to the Cedi Phu khau thong
It soars high into the haze of the sky.
It lies in the midst of fields surrounded by brightness and calm.

Boats mess around in clear water.
A lawn spreads from the base to the steps.
It is surrounded by water which is its boundary.
Cedi and Wihan together constitute a large Wat which
in this province looks like a fortification.
The Cedi towers in polygonal structures.
The monument is graded upwards in three sections
Ways of access are at all four sides. Oh peaceful grandeur!

His poem of proverbial character, *Sawatdi raksa*, attained a fairly large circulation. It is one of the 'lesser works' of Thai literature—both in volume and aesthetic value. Nevertheless, this *suphasit* poem is invariably included in all textbooks of Thai literary history or at least mention is made of its title. In fact, the poem has a significance for Thai cultural history that is in inverse proportion to its volume. Within the compass of only 143 *klon* verses the more important rules that govern the conduct of everyday life are listed—rules which are only to a small extent inspired by the high spiritual precepts of Buddhism. The emotional and intellectual world of the average Thai is still focused on concepts of animism. The vicissitudes of Thai culture, which we are frequently confronted with, are also apparent in the verses of *Sawatdi raksa*. The almost manic tendency of systematizing everything to the minutes detail that is inherent in Indian culture is, to a certain degree, also evident in this poem. Do this in the morning and that at night, wear red cloth on Sundays, and gray cloth on Fridays. Such strict regulation on schematization does not harmonize with the natural awareness of life of the Thai and their artistic temperament which is, in fact, averse to all abstractions. By contrast, the artistic credo of the Thai is rather characterized by natural transitions, continuously variable fusion, by the merging of parts without any systematic breaks, and by a sequence of associations in fluid rhythms.

Sawatdi raksa does not contain revelations of significance; no great utterance and, apparently, no thoughts of great consequence. Most of what is said is also known from other sources. The poem contains some worldly wisdom and maxims which seem contradictory to the exhortations and advice which appear side by side and are seemingly based on nothing other than superstitions. e.g. (verses 8 pp.)

Do not forget to maintain happiness with zeal
in harmony with the precepts of the elders.

That is: early in the morning when rising
and chasing sleep away, do not be fussy or angry.
Turn your face east and south
and above water recite Buddhist scripture
in praise of the Three Refuges
altogether thrice, then wash your face.
Thereafter, speaking and utterance can be useful.
This will increase esteem and dignity as time goes by,
For the star protecting man's character lies in your face in the morning.

Extract, 48 pp.

Furthermore: in the easy hours of leisure
no woman should rest in your arms.
After love making you should take a bath.
Happiness will increase, dangers be dispelled.
Furthermore: washing your hair on Tuesday and Saturday will end
    misfortune.
Cutting your nails on Wednesday and Monday will avert misfortune.
All that (happens) on Thursday (will bring) happiness.

Furthermore: when taking a bath
in a river, waterway, in the wood, a grotto
look in the direction of the flow of the water,
turn your face in the direction of the flowing river.
It is forbidden to empty your bowels and relieve yourself in the water.
Do not turn your face against the stream of the water
lest the dirt (of the water) touch you.
After bathing is finished bow in praise of Phra Khonkha, the goddess.

Furthermore: knowledge of magic invocations is useful.
At night you must not forget to recite them.
They have a mighty effect against your enemies
increase your power and reputation.

When a watch dog barks or howls
do not curse him in coarse manner.

This would be detrimental to your grandeur, and dangerous
no one would ever respect your words thereafter.

The names of several other poets are associated with Sunthon Phu; poets who are said to have been his pupils or apprentices. At present, no proof can be furnished for such assumptions. Nevertheless, mention must be made of one poet, who presumably belonged to the inner circle of pupils around Sunthon Phu and is considered to have been his adopted son. His name is **Nen Klan** and it is quite likely that he is the author of *Nirat Nen Klan*. This *nirat* describes a journey from Bangkok to the Buddhist sanctuary Phra thaen dong rang in the vicinity of Suphanburi. The reader's attention must emphatically be drawn to this *nirat*. Its literary and aesthetic levels are on par with the works of Sunthon Phu. However, not one of the latter's poems compares with the freshness and naturalness of Nen Klan's narrative. With Sunthon Phu many a rhyme would have turned out smoother, and more elegant, but also in a more conventional manner. With Nen Klan nothing runs in the groove of routine. His powers of observation are acute and what he sees he expresses in his own distinctive style. He also displays a discriminating sensibility for the finer shades of meaning. The richness of his pictorial descriptions is amazing. When comparing verses (662) to (667), for instance, with a similar environmental description by Sunthon Phu, the author of this study would show preference to the verses of Nen Klan.

A possible deficiency of Nen Klan's poetry is the absence of lofty phrases, so-called 'golden words' that are the pride of every collection of proverbs, maxims and aphorisms. Nen Klan's personality, as reflected by his *nirat*, is too unpretentious to strive for brilliance by means of extraordinary diction or pointed emphases.

At the beginning of this *nirat* Nen Klan complains of his personal lot:

> Wat Liep had been reached. It is very cool.
> I see the houses and buildings of my grandfather .
> I see even those in which I formerly lived.
> I remember those times and tears come into my eyes in great profusion
> When grandfather was the Cau Khun Sun Sena
> I had no father. I was kept by the kindness of grandfather
> to provide eating and bedstead. He protected me.
> Those were times of perfect peace.
> My aunt also guarded me and provided shelter.

> The merit I make shall be transferred to aunt and grandfather
> so they may enjoy happiness in the abodes of heaven.
> May they enjoy happiness and peace throughout
> to the end of their mortal life.
> When grandfather died, only grandmother was left
> upon whom I was totally dependent,
> It turned out that she became angry, forsook me,
> dropped me like hot (iron).
> My God, what bad deeds must I have committed in my former life?
> Father and Mother, what bad luck, I have never seen.
> Thinking of the kind of misery that befalls me, blood flows from my eyes.
> I am an orphan, alone, moving hither and thither.
> But now I have found a place as a monk and begin to recover.
> I keep the rules as a novice, eating only in the forenoon.
> I do not violate the precepts of Buddha.
> I assign some of my merit to my (other) grandmother
> who nurtured me from her bloodstream
>   and helped to maintain me.

A great part of what Nen Klan describes is original and unique to the literature of his time. Verses (306 pp.) read thus: 'Clouds are towering and grow all around like a boundary. Some are green or red, mixed like on a decorated curtain....' Verse (590) is the starting point of a new narration within the poem, a true travelogue, a masterpiece of clarity and vividness. What in Thai poetry could possibly be compared with it? Nen Klan and his 'father' (Sunthon Phu) have almost reached their destination and are collected in the open country along the river bank:

> Relatives of the father's pupils advance to greet him
> and respectfully offer him the ox-cart.
> They are Chong, the younger brother of Kaew, and the Chinese Klin.
> They are familiar with the environs, with the forest paths.
> The ox-cart advances to receive us at the bank of the river.
> At nightfall father puts on all three (monkish) gowns.
> We mount the cart. A lantern is suspended in front.
> There are lateral divisions and a cover—it is all right.

Both of us youngsters sit inside,
the elder Nen sits in front under the cover.
Chong, the younger brother of Kaew is daring
he sits in front, and the Chinese Klin climbs in at the rear.
The cart moves noisily into the jungle
as if a conch horn were sounded at full blast.
There are sounds emitted such as ae—i, ae-ot
as if played on the strings of a *So* in melancholic sweet strains,
(The cart) bumps into a hole—causing a loud noise.
Branches rotting on the ground are cracking.
Liver, kidneys and bowels are shaken and jolted.
Stumbling, bumping, jolting and swaying
makes us giddy and drowsy in the head.
The lantern goes out and it is dim like in a cave.
We come near a pond and manage to pass by it with a vehement jerk
but Nu Tap and the elder Nen are used to driving in ox-carts.
They are not giddy, sit and laugh and spur the buffaloes.
Father sleeps calmly leaning against his seat.
He taught me to sway with the rhythm of the cart which prevents
    giddiness.
(Since) I know this, I am attentive and sit with ease.
I sway with the rhythm of the cart leaning against my seat.
The ox-cart continues to move slowly until deep into the night.
Animal voices ring out loudly—it is frightful
In the thick jungle tigers are snarling and roaring.
I perceive brightness—light like fire and
ask father whether ghosts appear as lights
to mislead us and make us turn in a circle.
Deep in the night I feel the movement of my spirit.
A tree goddess utters murmuring sounds.
The cart moves in a circle failing to move out of the swamp
until the buffaloes with a jerk forge their way out of it, puffing and
    blowing.
Fortunately, the good merit of father helped us all.

Eventually, the locality Takhe (verse 656) was reached—everybody is relieved and cheerful. They had escaped the dark of night and returned to civilization. The villagers contemptuously referred to as 'backwoodsmen' offer food to the guests. Poet Nen Klan, with the air of a city dweller, describes the scene as follows:

> We have reached Ban Takhe surrounded by thick brushes.
> Dark night,—I think it was four o'clock in the morning.
> We are allotted a large room in Chong's house for passing the night,
> Father is still praying in the ox-cart,
> When at daybreak the sky is clear
> I see fields, houses—they look as if painted in a picture.
> On the left side, at the edge of the fertile wood (stand)
> Teng, Takhien and many Rang trees on shady hills.
> On the right side, fields and gardens and a bamboo thicket.
> Flocks of parrots look for food in the hills.
> Peasants allow the buffalo herds to roam freely in the fields.
> Everything is so nice to look at and we feel at ease.
> The villagers, the backwoodsmen, offer us food.
> Curry, vegetables, sweets and *Pla ra* they offer.
> They also offer lizards, spiders and ox-frogs baked in their skin.
> Both men and women of these backwoodsmen are naive —
> in addition, *Pla thu* and crabs from the woods prepared in the poor people's way.
> They have no betel nuts, (therefore) they collect all kinds of bark and put them in trays,
> in order to offer them to us monks, in so doing they wish to gain merit for themselves.
> Only reluctantly do we eat the produce of the woods and not vomit.
> But Nu Tap, Phi Nen and myself, we look at the frogs,
> the lizards and spiders and turn away nauseated
> and our nausea will not end.

In the opinion of Thai literary historians another poet, who lived in the early part of the nineteenth century, stands out. His works are included in the curriculum of all Thai schools. His name is **Poromanuchit Chinorot** and he was a son of Rama II. The poet lived from 1780 till 1853. He entered the monastery at the early age of twelve and remained a monk until the end of his life. Quite obviously the

The Bangkok Period, 1782–1932

leisurely atmosphere of monastic life was conducive to his comprehensive and varied literary creations.

Poromanuchit was the type of a *poeta doctus*. Consequently, much of his literary work is understandable only to those who, like him, were familiar with Pali and Cambodian. His verses abound with words from these languages, presumably foreign words in his time, and which to a great extent have presently become loan-words. It was because of the use of such vocabulary that Poromanuchit chose for his poems a metre that of all metres available was the least commensurate to a monosyllabic isolating tone language like Thai. The *kham chan* borrowed from Indian prosody indeed requires polysyllabic words rich in consonants. Hence, it was necessary for him to use, above all, words of Sanskrit, Pali or Khmer origin.

The work of this author which is best known up to the present time is the historic epos *Taleng Phai*, 'The Vanquished Burmese', which describes the struggle of the Thai under Naresuon (1590–1605) against the Burmese. The climax of this historic event was the duel between Naresuon and the Burmese crown prince who was defeated and slain. This is the gist of Poromanuchit's epos. But, even in this poem the greater part of the verses deal with the description of the environment. The march of the Thai troops through woody areas is used by the poet to describe at length the fauna and flora in addition to the preceding description of the military uniforms and armament.

Other literary creations of Poromanuchit are varied and, in the frame of the present study, can only be indicated. His *suphasit* poem *Kritsana son nong*, 'Krishna Teaches his Daughters,' and smaller works such as 'Songs for Calming Elephants' are well known. Poromanuchit also composed Buddhist poems, a 'Chronicle of Ayutthaya', a handbook about astrology and a treatise about the *chan* metre which has been used by poets up to the present time; and also a number of works in Pali, for instance, *Pathama Sambodi*, 'the life of Buddha.' He also completed—by one third of its total volume—the unfinished poem *Samuthakhot* which dates from the reign of Phra Narai.

The reign of the first three rulers of the Cakri dynasty (1782–1851) was an extraordinarily productive period in Thai literature. There is a considerable number of other poets of this period who are still known and have left us larger or lesser works. However, only a fraction of such works have been exposed to the western audience through translations. Even in present-day Thailand poets such as **Nai Mi, Khun Phum, Khun Suwan, Chaiwichit, Bamroe Borirak, Kraisonwicit,**

Phuwanet Narin, Isaranuphap are only known to a small circle of literary connoisseurs. Their works comprise *nirat* poems, eulogies of kings and of the country and some smaller texts which are of significance for poetology. Today only two poets are known to the larger public: **Detchadison** and **Maha Montri**.

Nai Mi's biographical details are not known, and it may be ruled out that they will ever be known. It is evident from his *Nirat Suphan*, which is responsible for his fame as a poet, that he journeyed from Bangkok to Suphanburi in 1844 or 1845 during the reign of Rama III (1824–1851), but the journey was probably continued under Rama IV (1851–1868) and Rama V (1868 onwards).

For the present-day reader *Nirat Suphan* is not only a poem, but also an official report in poetic form. He describes in detail the execution of his mission of collecting taxes in the town and province of Suphanburi. Originally, the purpose of *nirat* was to express a yearning for one's far away beloved, but this aspect plays only a marginal part in *Nirat Suphan*. The verses expressing yearning appear to be incidental and read like the records of a public notary. His *nirat* already foreshadows the end of this literary genre.

Nevertheless, *Nirat Suphan* is pervaded by a poetic atmosphere reminiscent of the blossoming of *nirat* poetry in Thailand. It has been asserted that Nai Mi may possibly have been a pupil of Sunthon Phu. If so, he certainly was a master-class student. As a whole Nai Mi's poems are of a more austere character, but they also show traits that go beyond Sunthon Phu: the frame of action is altogether consistent and terse, the plot logically structured and well thought-out. He does not use clichéd phrases—which are manifested in some of Sunthon Phu's verses to the point of embarrassment—and avoids trivial or unpoetic images solely used in order to achieve appropriate rhymes.

As it is typical of a *nirat* poem, Nai Mi records his arrival at different legs of his journey from Bangkok to Suphanburi. He almost completely avoids personal lamentations. Objective reports prevail throughout. Without any fantastic ornaments he reports what he considers remarkable in the places he visits. In as far as the former monk in him comes out, i.e., a tendency to teach and advise, he makes his insights known dispassionately and without any admonitions. As a whole the poem is full of allusions which today afford interesting insights into the economy of his time, the tax system, questions of sociological and even literary significance. In these spheres the *Nirat Suphan* is a veritable treasure house. His detailed descriptions of the practice of tax collection in ancient Thailand afford an insight into the life of the Thai as it actually was. He gives an unadulterated report and hands down his experiences in such a vivid and comical way which, in all Thai literature, can be found only with Maha Montri. There is the case of a man who refuses to pay taxes and 'escapes' (783 pp.). His wife, however, remaining at home—ironically described as a widow—knows a way out. She takes a lover who has a warrant of tax exemption, for such a 'document is tantamount to a fence which protects the fields.' Some clients do not even shrink from pairing their own daughters in order to obtain tax privileges. The latter event is described by the poet in a verse full of ridicule. The tax collectors thus become 'relatives' and (by begetting the daughters with child) 'help the family to grow.'

Maha Montri is akin to Nai Mi in some respects, in others he is of even greater importance. An insignificant number of his works have been preserved and in the official books of Thai history of literature he occupies only a marginal place; of his biography only a few uncertain dates are known. Nevertheless, his name is included in every, even the shortest, survey of Thai literature. The modest reputation he could gain—it is often represented in too modest a way—is based at least on one of his works: the *Bot lakhon ruang Raden Landai*.

The biography of the poet can be outlined in a few sentences. The dates of neither his birth nor his death are known. He is considered to have lived during the 'third reign,' i.e., from 1824 until 1851. Still, his name is not mentioned in the 'Chronicle of the Third Reign' written by Cau Phraya Thiphakarawong. Apparently he did not belong to the Greats of his age. This can also be concluded from his title Phra Maha Montri. The title designates an official, probably within the Ministry of Justice, who was of a rank which was secondary to that of Maha Thep. The honorific *phra* was conferred upon every incumbent of the office. It is the fourth grade of a possible seven. His personal name *sap* means 'wealth'.

Although we have no precise dates that could throw light on Maha Montri's life history his works offer clues to his personality and character.

He was, to a large extent, personally independent of the conventions of his time and had an original and creative mind. If we assume that this creative period spanned three decades, from 1820 until 1850, we can plainly see that his work should be rated as a unique achievement. He was a master of wit and irony, even delicate mockery. As a son of the people, familiar with human weaknesses which he found pardonable, he characterizes his protagonists in an endearing way which was not in the least bit judgmental. Was he a sage? Not quite, he was not perfect, which again was a good asset to his poetic contributions. There is a shady story about the manuscript of his poem *Phleng yau wa phra maha thep pan*; a high ranking courtier is so vehemently ridiculed in it, that the manuscript was confiscated.

Altogether four titles have been preserved under the poet's authentic name, viz. *Khlong ruesi dat ton, Konlabot kop ten sam ton, Bot lakhon ruang Raden Landai* and *Phleng yau wa phraya maha thep pan.*

In his *Phleng yau wa phraya maha thep pan* he severely criticizes a high ranking official named Phraya Maha Thep. We can scarcely imagine, in today's context, what measure of courage was necessary to write so critically in a closed society structured by strict hierarchical ranks. Fortunately for the poet, the Phraya Maha Thep was hated by many people at that time. Nevertheless, the manuscript was confiscated. Still, as Prince Damrong, a later editor, writes 'there were many people who copied the text.' With words of irony Maha Montri describes the traits of this 'dignitary':

> It is no accident that he enjoys a high standing,
> It is evident that in this country none is equal
> to this dignitary, neither man nor woman.
> He possesses everything, rank, reputation and wealth.
> By the Chinese he is feared more than the royal treasurer.
> In a former life he enjoyed the favor of Luong Chi.
> His wealth is astonishingly great.
> He is admired for his merit and called 'princely Lord'.
> But he is almost as cruel as a demon of Makasan . . .
> . . . his wisdom penetrates even the earth.
> His consummate cleverness should be praised.
> People outside are just talking, but they have never seen him personally.
> When he still was plain Thong Pan, (hence) they are doubtful.
> But I have clearly seen through things
> I was very close to him—and was afraid to be subject to him.

The subject matter of the poem *Raden Landai* breaks away from tradition and does not fit in with any Thai literary framework prior to 1830, following right to the present. Yet, the thematic material of the *nirat* is mostly taken from real life. However, this is rather by way of a weak imitation of the themes that are traditionally predominant in Thai literature. Traditionally, the action is set in 'higher' spheres (as distinct from a bourgeois-proletarian setting), in the world of gods, kings and potentates, in the realm of magic or imagination, not to mention specifically religious poetry. Reports (*nirat*) about military campaigns are puffed

The Bangkok Period, 1782–1932

up as eulogies or describe irrelevant details, but do not represent what is essential, for instance, the barbarism of the actual fighting. Behind many well-sounding rhythmic words the reality of things that should have been conveyed by the verses fades away.

There are only a small number of poems that do not conform to the frame outlined above: a few lines in the work of Cau Fa Thamathibet and some in that of Sunthon Phu; however, the 'peculiarities' of these poets do not really transgress set rules.

Bot lakhon ruang Raden Landai is the first realistic poem in Thai literature that is set in a bourgeois-proletarian environment. Moreover, Maha Montri gives his poem the air of a farce. He steps down from Mount Olympus. For him the unwritten canon of Thai literature had lost its validity and no longer represented the sublime and heroic, thereby devoting itself to the teaching of moral precepts and what was beautiful. He takes a step further by turning the farce into a critical and comic parody occasionally transgressing the borderline to satire. He uses parody as a means of criticizing the cultural life of his time.

Raden Landai, the hero of the story, is likened to *Inau* (verses 30) and Pradae is compared with Butsaba (verse 638). In fact, *Bot lakhon Raden Landai* is a parody of *Bot lakhon Inau*—this is an unprecedented novelty, the like of which did not exist in Thai literature before the time of Maha Montri.

Of all great epics—or more formally *bot lakhon* texts—*Inau*, based on Javanese Panji tales, is the least significant with regard to content. It is a story of love and adventure set in a court environment. The hero Inau dashes from one rendezvous to another. Eventually, he not only marries beautiful Butsaba, but nine princesses in addition. (Difficile est satiram non scribere).

It is assumed that Maha Montri deliberately chose the epos *Inau* for his parody. Apparently, this poem was largely known and widely circulated under Rama II and Rama III with the result that everybody interested in literary studies could naturally understand the parody. Moreover, in parodying this poem, he did not run the risk of offending national or religious sentiments. By way of contrast, it would have been unthinkable to subject to ridicule any figure from the *Ramakien*. After all, the contents of *Inau* are so naive and simple that a person devoted to what is aesthetically pleasing could not understand why just his type of literature met the approval of the reading public.

The poem *Raden Landai* was not only conceived as a parody of *Inau* taken as a whole, but also as a parody of minor details. The shaky hut of the protagonist or the shack of Pradu are hyperbolized as 'castles', the other persons of the cast—a mendicant musician and a cattle breeder—are variously described as 'Majesty', 'All Powerful', 'High justice'. Besides the parricidal meaning of such expressions another aspect should be noted.

Taking account of the literary production of the Thai up to the time of Maha Montri it is scarcely an exaggeration to say that with the poems *Raden Landai* and *Phleng yau wa phraya maha thep pan*, Thai poetry has become an independent third power (in Jacob Burckhardt's sense) apart from the state and religion. The present author is, however, rather hesitant to substantiate this thesis because Maha Montri's initiative has not been followed for many decades. There is also some hesitation since *Bot lakhon ruang Raden Landai*, as a purely poetic creation or aesthetic phenomenon, does not rank among the most important works of Thai literature. But, it is almost certain that in Maha Montri's mind the poem was not conceived primarily as an autonomous work of art for art's sake, but rather in line with Friedrich Schiller's doctrine (The Artist is a medium for leading man to truth and insight.) The fact remains that a highly independent mind in the year 1830 composed verses that stand out as a milestone in Thai literature, verses that were not written to serve either state or religion but to give expression, even in the form of a farce, to the belief in human values, truth, and ideals beyond any institutions.

Let us comment further on Maha Montri's critical faculties. His parody does not merely aim at provoking laughter, but rather lays bare a great many sore points of the rigid and lifeless conventions of his time. Yet, the poet did not behave as if he were a revolutionary. In fact, life in the society of his time was for him worth living—even as a penniless musician. With a contented air Raden smokes his pipe in front of his ramshackle hut, (493 pp.), (720 pp.). The poet does not make any accusations. He rather aspires to superior ideas proclaiming that everybody, even a cow tending Hindu and a migrant musician is a *phra ek*, a being equal to the Highest, to the Majesty within his own sphere of existence.

He does not proclaim a principle of absolute equality though—nothing could be further from the delicate mind of a Thai. The realistic description of Raden's and Pradu's environment is expressed in such language as to give the reader a feeling of cozy comfort. In spite of all poverty and wretchedness of their material circumstances of life—leaking roofs, rotting roof ridges, provisions sufficient only for a day, quarrels over the smallest sum of money—the protagonists are at ease in their dwellings and feel like kings. They enjoy happiness without being conscious of it. This, of course, is the happiness of the simple-minded. They are not humiliated by their poverty and low status. On the contrary, the boastful but inoffensive way of his speech and the levity of his character, evincing at times

The Bangkok Period, 1782–1932

Bohemian traits, go to prove that a certain haughtiness was not unfamiliar to him—a haughtiness of the simple-minded.

As borne out by the above outline of his personality Maha Montri is firmly grounded in the culture of his time and Theravada Buddhism. Social criticism is not his concern. In his poems he merely aims at exposing to ridicule the *literary* fashion prevailing under Rama III and to scoff at personal weaknesses (as in *Phleng yau wa phraya maha thep pan*). A simple hut of low class people may well be a 'castle'. And, praising with ecstatic words the physical charms of his beloved is not a privilege of Inau, the beautiful youth of royal descent, but it is the natural right of every beggar like Raden who, infatuated by the beauty of Pradae, praises her charms in such a way that her 'breasts sagging like empty bags, shriveled and withered like boiled cucumbers,' (73 pp.) are, in his imagination, 'of voluptuous fullness and firm like roasted bananas' (697).

Is his poem perhaps a praise of 'the simple life'? (cf. 766) Not at all, and certainly not in the sense of simplicity being the ideal form of life. In a few instances, Maha Montri even censures the weakness of his heroes and points in no uncertain manner, to their material needs, (19), (263), (521 pp.), (536), (570 pp.) etc.

What he tries to express is that in poetry there is, besides the environment of court and imagination, also the environment of plain human beings.

Maha Montri depicts his time, or rather aspects of it, as he sees them conditioned by his temperament. He tells his story in an almost Breughlian manner: with incorruptible sincerity which is revealing in some places. But, he is always anxious to avoid any tendency that could be interpreted as being detrimental, or destructive to, the existing social order. He is not inspired by a naive faith in progress or by a missionary zeal but, rather, by a hope of gradual change. In him there is no trace of unbridled fanaticism. It is clear that a poet of such profound humanity whose thoughts are rooted in the whole of human existence cannot conceive his works from the viewpoint of someone 'disillusioned' or 'in despair.' He is aware that life, at any moment, is fraught with all kinds of defects and shortcomings. In Maha Montri there was a certain aloofness towards his time and his 'heroes.' Hence it can be said that his irony was objective.

In point of style, Raden Landai is essentially different from *bot lakhon* poems of previous times. It is obvious that the poet does not simply want to ponder in beautiful, euphonious verses but that he is intent on conveying a message through them. Hence, his verses are terse and well thought-out. Almost every verse follows up the thought of the preceding one or introduces a new idea. Verbal flourishes are completely absent and there is no accumulation of synonyms which in former epics stretch over several lines merely to describe the 'beauty' of 'Sida', for instance.

> I shall give an account about
> poor Raden Landai
> who, sole ruler of himself, saunters
> along the market place near the 'Big Swing' in front of the temple of Brahma.
> He lives in a castle—with thin pillars and a broken top.
> A buttressed wall surrounds the palace, made of spiny thorns.
> He has soldiers, howling and barking, they tell the hours
> waiting to destroy malicious enemies.
> With his fiddle moving from one house to another begging for some rice
> which is offered to him as sustenance for life.
> No one hates him, neither woman nor man, some
> people submit themselves as to a Majesty.
> At nightfall when dusk descends
> mosquitoes come, he lights a smoldering fire, lies down
> to sleep on a bamboo mat instead of a diamond studded bed.
> The ruler of the earth becomes intoxicated with hashish.
> When sunrays arise at dawn
> he stoops over a basin to wash his face.
> He then eats the rice that remained stuck together with fish skin.
> He then proceeds to the river to take a bath.
> He dives three times to clean off the dirt and sweat.
> He goes up the steps and enters the room
> mixes perfume with white powder and
> rubs his cheeks and chin in the manner of cats
> fastens his trousers with an ornamental pin.
> (He wears) his 'heavenly cloth' of white colour
> as a belt with fringes (like) a scribe of the Lawa from Laos,
> All this looks like the beginning of a shadow play.
> He wears a wreath of nuts, his carrier-bag around his neck.
> He looks magnificent, even better than Panyi.
> In his hand he wields a club to ward off the dogs.

With his fiddle he proceeds on his way.
He reaches
a newly built town which looks marvelous.
In the center are the palace and pigsties.
A cowshed is at the side of the palace wall.
Prince Raden saunters through the gateway.
A pack of dogs threaten him in front and behind.
He brandishes his club to ward them off, but he does so in a trembling and clumsy manner.
His Highness straightens up his loin cloth ready for the fray.

Meanwhile
Dame Pradae, the most beautiful one,
when early in the morning Pradu, the ruler of the earth
leaves his palace to feed the cows,
still loiters in bed, elegant and idle.
She carefully cuts the hashish for her husband.
Then she takes a bath, powders herself and dresses
combs her hair, removes the lice, and binds her hair in a knot,
She hears faintly the barking of the dogs
supposing that the cows have entered the banana plantation.
She opens the window a little
and scolds angrily—but with a lady's voice —
when perceiving Raden Landai.
The beautiful lady turns away
nevertheless she stealthily looks at the man.
Behold! His is a body well-built!
More handsome than that of my husband!
No one in the whole town of Tani is on par with him.
Confused and enraptured by desire
the Dame full of amazement looks up to the king.

Meanwhile
His Majesty Landai, glittering with gold, looks into
the eye of the Dame from Tani.
The ruler of the earth looks at her attentively.
She is tall and slim, looks like a ship's rope.

> She is so beautiful—like a camel from Batavia
> Looking at her from head to toe—white are only her eyes.
> Her cheeks, both of them, are like the fruit of the Yo tree.
> Her eyebrows round like a spinning wheel
> her nose curved like a crooked knife,
> Her ears are hollow, her face disfigured,
> the base of the neck short and thick.
> Both her breasts sagging like empty bags.
> Shriveled and withered is her bosom like a dried cucumber.
> She chews betel paste between royal lips.
> She is indeed wonderful—the divine dame.
> Is she a daughter of the king?
> Or is she his spouse?
> Moved by love his heart throbs
> and he lets his golden fiddle sound forth.

As literary studies stand at present it can be safely assumed that **Khun Phum** was the first Thai poetess. It follows from *Phleng yau chaloem phra kiet*, her most important poem, that she lived during three reigns assuming her poetic activities under Rama III in 1824. She was an official at the court of Rama III and Rama IV (reigning from 1851 to 1868).

It emerges from verses (68 pp.) of the above quoted poem that she was obviously 'ordered' to write an obituary of Rama IV. In the light of the source material available, however, any further statements about her life history cannot be other than conjectural. In the afore-mentioned poem Khun Phum herself makes a few statements about her origin. Her 'father was an official of the Ministry of Finance,' (210) under Rama III. She refers to her father with the greatest of respect. 'He was an honorable man and on intimate terms with the King,' (216). This is a valuable indication that she was not originally of the lower class, but belonged to the privileged middle class for whose members it was easier to learn to read and write. She acquired these accomplishments presumably in her paternal home.

Strangely enough, Khun Phum was employed in the 'armory,' *phra saeng*, (639) and it is assumed that her position was that of a registry clerk. Verse (181) suggests that she might have been appointed court poetess—commissioned to praise first and foremost the ruling monarch.

In the light of her poem she can be characterized as a woman of resolute spirit who was not plagued with any doubts or scruples. Her books should be read in every home (660). What she has written down can not be found elsewhere; everything emanates from herself, (662). Besides, she does not hesitate to mention that her poems are actually read by the royal family and the courtiers (592 pp.). She goes on to describe herself as 'stubborn', (569). Apparently, she enjoyed the favor not only of the king but also of other high ranking members of the nobility, (570 pp.). All in all, she appears to have been a person with a positive attitude towards life and moral values. She puts her trust in this life which to her is not 'miserable'. She appreciates the 'purity and glory of life' and rejects its 'sins and lawlessness', (729 pp.). Nevertheless, she regrets 'being a woman' and in the life to come she would like to be 'a handsome man', (723 p). It follows that this resolute lady Khun Phum does not stand for the ideas and aims of the feminist movement.

By its nature, the content of *Phleng yau chaloem phra kiet* is of limited scope. As a eulogy the poem centers around the King and glorifies his life and actions. Despite the pre-set frame, Khun Phum manages to portray some other things as well, this is not only proof of her strong personality but also of interest to contemporary cultural historians.

The poem begins in praise of Rama IV, Mongkut, who died on October 1, 1868, (3 pp.). His demise is associated with supernatural phenomena, with a 'heavenly omen,' (6). There are certain auspicious astrological constellations on the day of his death. The propitious planet Jupiter approaches the moon, and at night 'the moon was darkened', (10) presumably not by an eclipse but as a result of a heavy cloud cover, (11). Alleged further events are relegated to the realm of the fable by the poetess herself. 'There were rumors,' (12), about a comet. Khun Phum reports all this in phrases difficult to interpret linguistically. Her hymn in praise of Rama IV is like 'blazing light,' (16), and she does not hesitate to compare the heavenly phenomena associated with the death of the King with those that took place when Lord Buddha died, (29), (this is presumably an allusion to the hour of death of the Buddha). Khun Phum literally reaches for the stars in order to praise the deceased ruler. She does this in hymned words which in fact captivate the reader by their rhythm and mood so that he can become one with the verses. One must read those passages slowly, line by line, in order to appreciate the profound sentiment of the poetess. Again and again she ventures upon new glorification's but in each case, makes it clear that it is not she but 'the people' who saw the phenomena, (26), (31). Nevertheless, the highly poetic verses that bemoan the dead ruler are very much her own. Even the gods of this world are mourning, (36)—even though she does not equate the King to them.

Thai Literature

The King 'since long had the ardent wish' that his son Chulalongkorn, then just fifteen years old, should succeed him (verses 51 p.) . It is open to question whether this is true, especially since the assertion cannot be based on historic sources. The available sources state that it was a council of elders who decided that Chulalongkorn should succeed his father. On the other hand, Khun Phum was perhaps so familiar with King Mongkut's innermost thoughts that she felt justified to write verse to that effect.

The poetess is familiar with Buddhist ideas about life and death, (57 p.) and it can safely be said that the mourning expressed in her verses is free of any sentimentality. 'Death will come to all of us,' (62), nobody and nothing can escape it, (63), (81). Carefree the King strode out into the night, (87), cheerfully his heart rose, (86).

The enumeration of the persons, things and facilities left by the king (91 pp.) should not be regarded as having been arbitrarily made. The poetess wants to portray what in Mongkut's life was part of his mind and the inner scope of his activities.

Her eulogy reads thus:

(Verses 262 to 287)

> He maintained the city of the Siamese in the state of a brilliant gem
> likewise the beautiful palaces, temples and sculpture.
> The king departed in order to dwell in heaven
> at three o'clock in the morning on a Monday in the fifth month.
> Somdet Phra Com Cakraphat became the (new) ruler
> mounted the throne as the highest king of his dynasty.
> His retinue entrusted the land to him
> and his duties according to Brahmanic law, wishing
> that he should follow the example of the highest of his dynasty
> who ruled the city and the country.
> A great blessing for the land. Music sounds
> it is abundantly decorated with wreaths and flowers.
> Every place is full of light, the houses of the Phraya so
> as if an upheaval would sweep the land.
> Somdet Phra Com prepares his reign.
> He preserved the living as hoped
> The great awakening was in heaven as on earth,

The Bangkok Period, 1782–1932

in the presence of Indra with the Apsaras of the spheres.
The sons of the gods, in the Dusit (heaven) reborn
are incarnated as dignitaries, in great numbers.
The queen possesses great wealth, nothing can hinder her.
Ever lasting and good are land, houses and towns.
This is the third great awakening and
together with death the fourth is (now) on its way.
In such a manner as to praise the Highest, the seat of virtue
it should be a place of joy.

Two further events that happened in the reign of Rama III must be mentioned because of their impact on Thai literary history. Firstly, the introduction of the letter press and secondly, the preservation of the greater part of poetic and scientific literature on stone slabs on the walls of Wat Phra Chetuphon (Wat Pho).

An Englishman called James Low brought the first printing blocks to Thailand. However, the letter press industry got its initial boost only in 1835 when a printing plant was established by the American Protestant Mission—this was a decisive step forward to a wider distribution of Thai literature. Even so, printed books of substantial size gained popularity only under the successor to Rama III.

Perhaps, many a text and poem would not be extant today if Rama II, on the occasion of the restoration of Wat Phra Chetuphon in Bangkok, had not implemented his plans and ordered the writers and scholars of his time to collect all literary and 'scientific' texts then known and have them chiselled on marble slabs. The greater part of the texts were works of literature proper, but they also included scientific findings of the pretechnical age, and texts about astrology and popular medicine.

Signs of a renovation of the literary scene became apparent in the reign of Rama IV, Mongkut, (r. 1851–1868). It is true that traditional subjects and forms still prevailed in stage plays, epic poems and songs but, during Mongkut's reign, Thailand changed its attitude of aversion towards western powers. As the first monarch of his country the King took up the study of English. Trade agreements were concluded with all important western states. A Thai diplomatic mission was sent to London in 1857. As a member of the delegation **Mom Ratchothai** wrote an account of the mission in his *Nirat London*. The metre employed in this *nirat* follows the tradition set by Sunthon Phu. The *nirat* of Mom Ratchothai although a travel account, does not contain a single line of lyrical verse. It is sober in content, and events are reported in a matter-of-fact protocol manner that resembles a diplomatic report rather than a poem. Mom Ratchothai rightly felt that the classic style of the *nirat* had outlived itself as a means of depicting events set in a technical environment.

The encounter with Lord Palmerstone in London reads as follows:

We then mounted a carriage to pay a visit to Lord Palmerstone	in cheerful mood and Lord Clarendon, the home secretary.
Upon our arrival we entered the building	and found ourselves in a shining hall of mirrors.
All around an ambiance of wealth pleases the eye.	We entered and sat down on chairs
Lord Palmerstone received the envoy of the Cakri in a cordial manner	He came in and shook our hands without condescension or pride.
In a colloquial tone he inquired about our plans	and the concerns that prompted us to approach him.
The envoy said in reply	that our sojourn here has been very pleasant so far
and that we have come now to take leave	since we want to return to Bangkok.
We conversed in a friendly manner	as friends do who appreciate each other.
The envoy took leave and went away	We strode straight-away to the carriage outside the palace
and proceeded to Lord Clarendon in the Admiralty.	The envoy broached his topics in very precise words.

He reached agreement about what he wanted.	There was joking on both sides and cheerfulness.
In the evening we were back at the hotel	and thought of Bangkok longingly and wistfully.
Everybody was discontented because the day of departure was not known yet.	We did not know how many days we had to pass.

Mongkut himself composed a series of poems in traditional style, in addition to a number of religious and historical treatises. The most significant remains of his literary endeavors are some four hundred decrees he issued, and which must be considered in the present survey making allowance for the fact that most Thai literary texts have come down to us fragmented. The vivid language of these legal texts is of greater interest to us than poems of secondary quality, quite apart from the fact that these legal regulations are a first class source of cultural history. Mongkut was anxious about such things as the price of rice, the composition of theatrical casts, the national currency, the ordination of monks, verbal spelling, correct policy operations, the appointment of judges and the fixing of the date of the Songkran festival. The collection of these legal decrees became famous, especially through announcements, as the one contained in decree No. 165 published in 1858 dealing with the freedom of religious worship and superstitious practice indicates:

'No just ruler will restrict the freedom of his people in choosing their religious faith through which they hope to find solace and salvation in their last hour and beyond.

There are many precepts shared by all religions, as for instance the explicit prohibition to kill, to steal, to commit adultery, to speak what is not true, to drink intoxicating beverages. Advice is likewise shared such as to repress anger, to be friendly and truthful, to practice gratitude and generosity and many more good deeds which mankind, of whatever race or language, consider to be conducive to goodness, truth and righteousness.

Nevertheless, some individuals, in exercising freedom of religious worship, commit action's incompatible with the dictates of a good state government, even if such actions are considered praiseworthy by those who have lost their sense of judgment, or who have been misguided to believe in the righteousness of their actions by false reports or hearsay, or through the brainless and erroneous preaching of some bad monks who do not know the Tripitaka. . . . Among such malpractices is, for instance, the act of self-immolation by burning in veneration of the Triple Gem, or the dedication of one's decapitated head to the Buddha as a sign of veneration, or the sacrifice of blood from wounds inflicted upon one's own body. . . .'

Other poets of the period who are less well-known today are **Wongsathirat, Si Sunthon Wohan** and **Pin Klau**.

Apart from the well-known names preserved in books of Thai literary history there are a great number of anonymous poets who have left us relatively significant works; of particular importance is one poet who is the most frequently quoted today in Thai literature: The collection of sayings *Suphasit son ying*. 'A didactic poem for young women.'

The translation of the word *suphasit* as 'didactic poem' characterizes its scope and content. The original meaning of the word in Sanskrit and Pali is 'an auspicious utterance.' In view of the wide and diverse interpretation of the term *suphasit* it may be rendered as proverb, aphorism, maxim, saying and, more generally, as a wise and witty utterance.

The fact that the content of the *suphasit* tends to be of a didactic or moralizing nature can be explained by the historical literary origin of these poems. One may safely assume that *suphasit* poems were modeled on the numerous verses of Buddhist code—or general moral content—which were interspersed in the widely diffused canonical and extra-canonical writings evident since the Sukhothai period, e.g., such writings as the Gathas and Jatakas and the well-known compilation of verses, the *Dhammapada*. It may also be assumed that the *Pancatantra*, or the book of fables of the Indian classical period which contained many sayings in metric form, was known in Thailand at an early date. Above all, however, it appears that *Lokanithi*, a work written in Pali, has had a decisive influence on Thai *suphasit* poetry.

Based on the aforementioned works *suphasit* poems of various content and size were also composed in Thailand, beginning with *Suphasit Phra Ruong* which was presumably written in the course of the thirteenth century. However, the *Suphasit Phra Ruong*, on the one hand, and the *Suphasit son ying*, on the other, each belong to a different literary type, as is evident by a comparison of the two. The *Suphasit Phra Ruong* comprises partly of collected, and partly of created sayings which are either loosely strung together or not coherent at all, whereas the *Suphasit son ying* is a coherent poem that follows a deliberate plan expounding, in its various sections, didactic rules and moral teachings. What both *Suphasit Phra Ruong* and *Suphasit son ying* have in common are merely a few thematic aspects. Owing to the equivocal meaning of the word *suphasit* it is imperative in each individual case to clearly define which liteary type a given poem belongs to.

The poem *Suphasit son ying* contains lyrical as well as epic elements. Part of the poem, in as far as it belongs to the aphoristic type, could be characterised as philosophic poetry. Analyzed holistically, however, the poem is not so much the concise expression of coherent thoughts based on a lyrical I—a personal inner entity—but rather an enumeration of hard facts and objective observations presented in versified form. The epic element is, of course, predominant. The present author would hypothetically classify the poem as belonging to the didactic category.

For a long time the authorship of the poem was attributed to Sunthon Phu. However, in the light of recent literary research, and weighty arguments advanced against this theory, the assumption can no longer be adhered to.

With a sense of humor, sometimes even with cynicism, the poet offers advice from his vantage point of wisdom.

> As to the eyes: do not let them roam around too much.
> Yet you must heed signs and their meaning.
> When meeting all the young men
> do not look sideways, shut your eyes, do not stare at them.
> Your eyes will lead you astray and you will fall into disrepute.
> Likewise, if you give a sign to impart your thoughts.
> True or untrue, people will gossip (about you),
> bad people will say with contempt that your eyes are covetous.

> It is true that, as a rule, women and men attract each other
> by no means do they want to thwart a way which is so fitting.
> When you fall in love, do so in secret
> do not show your love openly or you will be put to shame.
> Behave like a tree that bends with the wind
> freely moving, but does not break its branches.
> Resist, see to it that things turn out well
> behave like a *Camari* tree and be careful to protect your body.

Noble lady, liken yourself to a lotus blossom
try and keep your head above water.
Spread the scent of blossoms in the air
nothing can keep the bees from longing and hoping.
(However) once mating is ended as wished for (by the male)
he boastfully departs, free of desire.
He does not stay on to exchange caresses (with you),
he roams about to try it with others.
Lo! the hearts of men are all alike.

More sober in diction but more unequivocal in content is the poem *Owat kasatri*, 'A Warning to Women' of which the author is unknown:

At bed-time try all you can to please him.
Admire your husband at his feet as best you can.
Do all the things he likes.
Stay up until he falls asleep. Then prepare everything carefully.
Fetch water and wait on him who is your husband when
in the morning he wants to wash his face.
Beautiful lady, bear all this in mind!
Prepare betel and good cigars
and offer them to him in the customary order.
Eating and sleeping,—that is what counts!
Be observant and never be indifferent.
(Serving) fragrant and sweet things is the task of all beautiful women.
Do not neglect him trusting that other people will take care (of him).
A good woman, in general, has good manners.
What she takes in hand will be clean, nothing is (done) in haste.
You should be interested in good things wherever.
Your speech should be soft, never offensive.
Attend to your household and be active.
Even when you have done what he (usually) likes but if he says he does
    not like it, be silent.
Control yourself, fear what is wrong, be attentive.
Conduct yourself in such a way that people admire you.
Keep in mind the telling words of this teaching
good for all serviceable spirits, live up to it.

All your heart's striving be calm and composed.
Do not aspire to what is sinful and do not wish for it.
The Canon has it that there are four kinds of good women.
We shall not pass over them in silence but expatiate on them
explaining them and pointing out their importance.
They should be looked into according to Buddhist teachings.

A new era was ushered in, both in politics and Thai literature, with the ascent to the throne in 1868 of King **Chulalongkorn, Rama V**. Prose writing began to win ground and the subject matter of poetry was, increasingly, more closely related to reality. The growing influence of the West and the more wide-spread elementary and higher education of the population played their part in this development.

The first National Library was founded in 1905, the foundation of the Siam Society followed in 1907. The latter played an important part in preserving and disseminating the literature of the country—its journal is one of the most important literary periodicals even today. A little earlier, in 1884, a new periodical appeared; it was titled *Wachirayan* and published old texts as well as new literary contributions.

Of the works of Rama V only certain parts can be classed as literature proper. Important sections of his work belong to what is known as professional and technical literature.

Bot lakhon Ngo Pa, the 'Negritos (of southern Thailand)', a text adapted to the stage, by its form and style still belongs to traditional schemes, but by virtue of its content it is something quite new. The setting of the plot is among the Semang, a small group of negritos living in the jungles of southern Thailand. It is a stage play in a Romeo and Juliet setting, a drama of jealousy and revenge with a tragic ending, which leads to the death of both lovers and the avenger. The description of the marriage rites and the customs of the Semang and of their natural environment is closely related to factual reality.

From a purely poetic point of view *Bot lakhon Ngo Pa* is a great success but it is also a turning point reflecting the contemporary intellectual situation of Thailand.

The prose works of Rama V are varied and of extensive scope. Mention must be made, first and foremost, of *Klai Ban*, 'Far Away from Home,' and *Phra ratcha phiti sipsong duan*. *Klai Ban* is a collection of letters which Chulalongkorn addressed to his daughter Nipha Naphadala during his second tour of Europe in 1907. In them he gives a vivid and detailed account—long-winded and digressive in places—of what impressed him most about the country and the people drawing comparisons with the situation in Thailand.

His letter dated August 9, 1907, for instance, gives an account of his encounter with emperor William II in Kassel:

> 136 th night
> Residential castle, Land Hesse-Kassel
> Friday, 9 th August R.S. 126

In the morning at eight o'clock I left Berlin. Only Boriphat and a number of officials accompanied me. Other dignitaries stayed a further night and then went straight-away to Paris. Horse carriage and railway were specially placed at my disposal. Since I left Berlin a few pages were in attendance near me all the time.

The country around Berlin does not look very fertile. The soil in sandy. Hence, pine-trees are thriving and rye is cultivated in the fields. As we move on the soil is getting better and there are many vegetable fields coming into sight. Near the border of Hesse-Kassel there are ranges of hills of moderate height. The hills are covered by woods up to their peaks. Below (the wooded area) are fertile fields. It is a pleasant sight, fields everywhere on the slopes.

The town of Kassel lies in the midst of a farming area, the castle Wilhelmshohe is located on a hill. You can see it from afar. The train was early and had to stop for a while. The station is located not in the town center proper but somewhere between the center and the castle Wilhelmshohe. The Emperor came to receive me. He was dressed in 'simple uniform' and sported a Thai decoration but wearing only the star around his neck without the chain. He wore the decoration according to German custom, not in the manner as did his adjutant General W.P. The Emperor said the General held the rank of a colonel at the time when he was only a major. The General had steadily advanced and at present holds the rank of inspector of the rifle arsenal. He is an expert of rifle weaponry. Were also present: the major, the first and second secretaries and the commander of the military district. After the presentation of both sides was over the Emperor handed me a special decree by which he gave permission to receive Boriphat into the ranks of the guards regiment No 4, Empress Augusta. He was also permitted to wear the regimental uniform.

Then we were conducted to the motor-car and mounted. The imperial automobile has seventy horsepower, it is white and looks superb. The front seats are covered by a roof, the rear is open. It has various accessories and emblems which were specially made for the Imperial car to give it an official appearance. In the glass division to

The Bangkok Period, 1782–1932

the front there is a round window that can be opened and shut. Hence, in order to communicate with the driver it is not necessary to lean out or use a megaphone. The Imperial pennant is fixed on the radiator. The horn emits a threefold signal to announce the Emperor's approach in a suitable manner. Each of the front lamps is decorated with a crown. Crowns are also applied to the rear of the car. The driver wore an arm-band and nice epaulettes on his shoulders. On our drive from the station only two persons were aboard the car. The inhabitants loudly cheering stood alongside the road leading to the castle hill. We drove around the castle and entered through the back entrance. The Empress, a princess and two elderly ladies in attendance received us in the hall. Both ladies have been the assistants of the queen for a long time. I was told they had been in the Imperial service for the last twenty-six years . . . .'

The accounts continues in this strain for several hundred pages.

In all the European countries he visited, the King met monarchs, princes and ministers, most of them celebrities. King Chulalongkorn's European tour was of the utmost political importance considering the fact that the autonomy of his country was menaced at the time especially by France.

The second work of great interest to cultural history, *Phra ratcha phithi sip song*, 'Royal Ceremonies During the Twelve Months (of the year)' describes in great detail the ceremonies held at the royal court of ancient Thailand. Moreover, mention must be made of a sizable number of other prose works of Chulalongkorn such as travel accounts, diaries etc.

During the reign of Rama V and after him works continued to be written about themes and in forms following classical literature especially *nirat* and *phleng yao* poems, boat songs and eulogies. Within the scope of the present survey, however, we can mention only the names of some of the more important poets such as **Sathit Damrong**, **Narit**, and **Phitayalap**. Mention must also be made of authors who left behind important historical works in the last century, e.g., **Thiphakarawong** and **Prachakitcakoracak**.

In the year 1910, Thailand's great king Chulalongkorn was succeeded by his son **Wachirawut, Rama VI** (r. until 1925). Politically, he was the most ineffective ruler of the Cakri dynasty, but, culturally, he transformed the residence of the Thai kings into a seat of the light muses. He had his own stage plays performed by his favorites. He was easily accessible to people who were beneficial to his own literary ambitions showing them great flattery. Wachirawut left a literary oeuvre of more than 120 books in addition to numerous essays. During his fifteen-year-reign, it appears that he could hardly have had sufficient time to attend to the business of actually ruling the country. At the end of his reign Thailand found herself on the verge of bankruptcy.

Wachirawut studied at Oxford and was later admitted to the cadet school at Sandhurst. He mastered English and had some knowledge of Latin and Sanskrit. He translated some of the plays and sonnets of Shakespeare into Thai; these translation are sympathetic and couched in beautiful language. The King composed fifty-four stage plays of his own, partly in traditional style, partly following western patterns. Their subject-matter is both traditional as well as based on a modern realistic background. The King also introduced the short story and the essay as new genres in Thai literature. He used his essays as a vehicle to spread his political—especially nationalistic—ideas which, during the course of the following years, had disastrous consequences. Confused by favor—and hate of the parties—his personal profile is variously interpreted in history. The same also applies to his literary works—*mutatis mutandis*. Apart from many writings that will remain worth reading, a number of works are full of empty pathos and bloodless poetry. There is for instance his 'Boat Song about the Nostalgia for Books.' As implied in the title, it is a dreadful verse:

> '... books made up in the fashion of modern times!
> A fashion I do not appreciate.
> They do not master the Thai language.
> The language of these modern times!
>
> Only cheap things appeal to our youngsters.
> As you read on you get mixed up in the head.
> They are out for destruction.
> A mad pattern, language contorted.
>
> I presume they imitate the foreigners.
> I am disgusted when reading, it is more than can be endured ....'

All intellectual activities in Thailand from about 1910 until 1940—and in many respects until the present—cannot be understood without considering the pioneering work of Prince **Damrong Ratchanuphap** (1861 to 1943). The prince, a son of Rama IV, accomplished outstanding and fundamental work in every field of the humanities, including the history of art and culture, in the Thailand of his

The Bangkok Period, 1782–1932

time. The full scope of his work can only be given in outline in this study. His activities as editor of literary texts hitherto unknown is almost as important as his own writings. For each text he wrote introductory notes which for us today often are the only clue for establishing literary dates. Thai historical research would be very skeletal indeed if it were not for the collection *Prachum Phongsawadan* founded by him, 'the collection of historical sources'.

Damrong was not a creative poet but a *homo literatus*, a man of letters, to whom Thai literature is indebted much more than to poets of secondary importance. Here are the titles of some of his works: 'Contributions to the history of *sepha* poems,' monographs on the 'songs for calming elephants', on particular poetic metres, on stage dancing, and his biography of Sunthon Phu, etc.

During the reigns of Rama VI and Rama VII (1925–1935) the literary work of at least two poets stands out from among a multitude of others, viz. Narathip and Phityayalongkon. Whereas the subject matter of the writings of Narathip, a son of Rama IV, adheres to the traditions of the old absolute monarchy—eulogies, historical accounts, ceremonies, the work of Phithayalongkon bears the mark of a transition.

It includes traditional verse poems besides prose writings, especially tales based on the real life of his environment. Phithayalongkon was also engaged as an active journalist who edited a newspaper and a periodical. His diction is conspicuous by its conciseness and simplicity.

Phithayalongkon's well known verse poems such as *Konok Nakhon* and *Sam Krung*, 'The City of Konok' and 'The Three Cities' are popular favorites even today. The first title is based on mythology. *Sam Krung* is a rather pathetic glorification of Thai history. An important prose work by the author is *Cotmai Cangwang Ram*, a collection of seven fictitious letters addressed by a father, living in a Thai province, to his son studying in England. The father offers advice on how a young gentleman should behave—a topic already dealt with several times in Thai aphoristic poems. But Phithayalongkon deals with the matter in his own peculiar way.

Another verse poem, *Samakhiphet*, written in the metre of *kham chan*, is a last attempt to create a didactic poem along traditional lines. Its author is **Burathat** (1892–1942). The poem is based on commentaries to the Buddhist scriptures. *Samakhiphet*, 'The Broken Concord' gives an account of an utopic realm in which concord finds itself destroyed by intrigues and thus falls victim to its enemies.

Khawiphot Thamaphimon (1858–1943) and **Khru Thep** (1877–1943) are two of the better known authors of the transitional period. The literary period after 1930, approximately, is generally referred to as the 'literature of the present.'

The Literature of the Present

The coup d'état of 1932, ending absolute monarchy in Thailand, has signaled a turning point in the development of Thai literature. The royal court is no longer the exclusive centre of all social and cultural life. A new upper class—independent of the nobility—has arisen, and a bourgeois middle class confronted by the pressing problems of modern times attempts to analyze them in literature. The mass media of newspapers and periodicals are at the disposal of a new generation. Writing and publishing is no longer a pastime of leisure hours, but has acquired the status of a profession.

The 'new generation', nevertheless, lives in the wake of traditional literature in as far as it is their primary concern to make the leisure of everyday life as entertaining as possible. Hence, at the outset a variety of popular fiction makes its appearance. Apart from a small number of titles these stories can only be categorized as literary trash.

Phu chana sip thit, 'A Victor in Every Direction' by **Yakhop** (pseudonym for **Chot Praphan**, 1904–1956) was one of the first popular novels with a wide circulation. It is mentioned here because of its high linguistic level: it is a story of love and heroism with a historical background. The novel has been imitated many times, for instance by **Mai Muang** (Pseudonym for **Kan Phuengbun**, 1898–1943) in his novel *Khun Sue*, 'The Victor.' He enlarged the story to fill several volumes. Again, the story centres around a glorious hero overcoming all adversities to win his beloved. However, Mai Muang could also write in a different strain—this is reflected in his creation of a new type of popular literature which in some respects has naturalistic features. It comprises essentially of novels and tales that describe the everyday life of the rural population, the environment of simple

The Literature of the Present

unsophisticated people. The uncomplicated action of the novel is told in simple and realistic language.

Manat Chanyong (1907–1965) published about 1000 titles; mostly tales set in a rural environment. However, his writings do not smack in any way of the 'blood and soil myth.' His protagonists are presented as naive but vital people in a rural environment who are able to cope in adverse circumstances in a spirit of equanimity and humor. The tales of Manat are typical of popular literature which, far from having any literary ambitions, entertain the reader in a lively manner. His story *Cap tai*, 'Captured Dead' was printed in Span, an Asian-Australian anthology in 1958.

The short stories of **Achin Pranchaphan** are also set in an environment of the common people. His best-known books appeared in 1966: *Sieng riek muang rae* and *Sawadi muang rae*, 'A Voice Calling from the Pit-head' and 'Good-bye Pit-head.' Both books are collections of short stories describing the hard life of the miners without glossing over anything.

The first generation of Thai prose writers came for a major part from the sphere of professional journalism. Under the circumstances prevailing in Thailand at the time these writers were involved only to a very marginal extent in political and social life. Under the military dictatorship of Phibun Songkran they scarcely had a chance to publish anything even remotely objectionable to the government. Hence, the literary production of this generation was, in its essence, limited to offering to the public articles written with a view to entertaining them. Their writings comprised not only rural tales, but also historical novels and, as a favorite for readers, novels about family life. The latter were mostly of the sob-story type: the deserted mistress, the ill-treated daughter-in-law, and the abandoned child. Such stories were often first printed in newspapers or periodicals and published in installments. It was not infrequent for authors to have had two or three novels published simultaneously in different periodicals under various pseudonyms. It is common knowledge that **Malai Chuphinit** has been published under ten different pseudonyms.

The literary production of Malai Chuphinit (who lived from 1906 to 1963) is indeed so comprehensive and varied in form that the use of the great number of pseudonyms seems plausible. Under the pseudonym Riem-eng he published mainly short stories that have today become one of the most popular literary genres. Chuphinit is the author of more than 2000 short stories. His *Chua fa*, 'To the End of the World,' has been adopted for the screen. Wealthy Pabo, a timber trader, marries a woman thirty years his junior. A love-affair arises between her and Pabo's nephew living in the same house. One day, the lovers were surprised by the appearance of Pabo in the middle of love-play when they were about to pledge fidelity for ever. With a cruel sense of consequence the cuckold made them fulfill their pledge. He unites them with shackles, leaving them otherwise untrammeled. Life thus becomes torturous for both of them. In response to their plea for clemency, Pabo merely hands them a pistol. The young woman shoots and kills herself; her lover stays beside her for a night until he finds a knife and manages to sever the hand of the woman still chained to him. He ends up in a state of madness.

Chuphinit published a series of hunting stories, *Long plai*, under the pseudonym Noi Inthanon—hunting and nature are depicted here in a realistic manner. His novels *Koet pen ying*, 'Born as a Woman,' and *Phaen din khong rau*, 'Our Land,' also won him great fame. Both novels published under his pseudonym Miaenong, are based on the same theme: clashes between the conservative, hierarchically structured society of old Thailand and the rising individualism adopted from the West. In other words, the inner conflict between convention and inclination which lovers fail to overcome.

The novel *Khang lang phap*, 'Behind the Picture' by **Si Burapha**, or **Kulap Saipradit** who was born in 1903, deals with a similar subject.

Sot Kuramarohit (born in 1903) belongs to the same generation. His work differs in essence from that of Si Burapha. His literary production not only aims at impartial and unbiased entertainment but is thoroughly imbued with an idealistic intention to reform Thai society.

Kuramarohit spent a few years in Peking studying the Chinese language and philosophy. With this background China is the scene of many of his novels. His novel *Paking nakhon haeng khuam lang*, 'Peking the City of Reminiscences!' has the character of an autobiography. A picture is drawn of the life story of a Russian woman who came to China as a refugee. Her only prop and support in a strange and hostile environment is her old father and a Thai student. Waraya is unable to cope with life in her environment and when her father senses that she is having an affair with the Thai student, he commits suicide as a warning that her love would only add to her suffering. Her friend returns to his homeland and, following her father's wish, Waraya enters a nunnery.

In his novel *Khon di thi lok mai tong kan*, 'A Good Man Rejected by the World,' the author depicts an idealistic-minded journalist who opposes corruption and abuse of power but is, nevertheless, doomed to failure. Likewise, his novel *Raya* deals with the failure of an idealist opposing meanness, craving for power

The Literature of the Present

and corruption. By setting up a model village community the author personally tried to carry out in his private life what he strove to bring about by his novels.

The work of **Dokmaisot** (pseudonym for **Buppha Nimamanamehin**, 1905–1963) deserves special mention. Dealing frequently with issues related to love and wedlock, her writing reflects thoroughly Buddhist attitudes and have thus been received in Thailand with much enthusiasm. Academic circles have made her works required reading in Thai universities. *Phu di*, 'Good people', is considered her best known novel. The central figure, Wimon, represents what Thais considered the 'perfect woman'—coping with her own life, as well as with that of others, with prudence, courage, endurance, strength of will, love and readiness to make sacrifices.

Literature in present-day Thailand is a picture of great variety. Apart from serious *belles-lettres* in good linguistic form there exists a mass of trashy popular fiction. However, two facts should be pointed out to characterize the present situation. Firstly, from among the more important authors the proportion of women is far greater than that of men and, secondly, subjects of social criticism are increasingly winning over subjects of *belles-lettres*. Naturally, there will always be an avid reading public for the novel of family life and the novel of adventure—with its fantastic heroic feats—but an increasing number of authors courageously brush aside many of the principles and taboos, they question traditional rules and deal with the conflicts of contemporary society and the failed attempts to resolve them. Such authors are **Sifa** (born in 1930), **Nithaya Natayasunthon** (born in 1925), **Kritsana Asokin** (born in 1931) and above all **Bunlua Kunchon** (born in 1911). **Tohyanti** (born in 1939) in her best-known novel *Roi monthien*, 'The Defilement,' did not even shun writing about the problems of Thai prostitutes and their sociological background.

Suwani Sukhontha (born in 1932) is another author who has already published remarkable books. She was justly awarded the SEATO literary prize in 1971. Her short stories and novels offer a sensitive depiction of people and nature. The preferred environmental context of her stories is the morbid lifestyle of a saturated bourgeoisie and the world of would be artists—most of them merely artist-craftsmen but believing themselves to rank among the great masters. The novel *Khau chue Kan*, 'His Name is Kan', has won the author a prominent place among writers of social criticism. Kan, an idealistic physician, makes up his mind to follow the path of maximum resistance. He runs a surgery practice in the lonely environment of a primitive rural setting. His wife, unable to cope with the challenging circumstances, returns to the prosperity of Bangkok. Kan, however, does not give up and continues to struggle against poverty and ignorance, but eventually fails to emerge victorious over the corruption of public servants. Kan is finally shot and killed. With her novel the author has stirred up a hornet's nest by fearlessly tackling in plain terms one of the worst problems of contemporary Thai society.

Rong Wongsawon (born in 1932) in his short stories not only turns his back on traditional literary subjects, but also tries to examine new linguistic forms of expression: fragmentary sentences, scraps of conversation, new-coined words, abbreviations, slang, and stringing together seemingly unconnected phrases. All this is tantamount to a radical break with conventional literary diction. In this new style Wongsawon has already a number of imitators and successors.

Khamphun Bunthawi transports his readers to the centre of northeastern Thailand, known as Phak Isan. His novel *Luk Isan*, 'A Child of the Northeast' is regarded in Thailand as the song of praise of the brave man of the common people. Khamphun's novel was declared the best narrative in 1976, and awarded the SEA.-Write-Prize in 1979. The novel is sure to win the reader's sympathy right away. It reads like a fairy-tale. Kun's family are law abiding and exhibit common decency in adverse situations, especially of material need. The novel has a tendency to idealize things but, at the same time, puts things in black and white. Malice and greed are associated with those who are not Thai nationals i.e., the Chinese and the Vietnamese who are mainly traders. The merit of the book lies largely in the matter-of-fact description of the adverse circumstances of the thirties.

Kham Phiphaksa by **Chat Kopchit** is a widely known novel which was awarded the SEA.-Write-Prize in 1982—it has also been translated into English and German. The author was born in 1954 in the province of Samut Sakhon.

Fak, the central figure of the novel, grows up motherless in a rural environment. He is, however, raised by a loving and caring father—a good-natured but simple minded school caretaker in his village. At an advanced age he marries a woman very much his junior. At his death Fak inherits both his father's position as school-caretaker as well as his wife. Very soon he is accused by the villagers, in a mean and humiliating manner, of entertaining sexual relations with his step-mother. All contrary affirmations of the idealistic-minded Fak are of no avail. His assertions are believed only by the village undertaker, a person held in very low esteem because of his trade. Fak's confidence in humanity receives a final blow when the religious rites on the occasion of his father's incineration were not attended by the villagers. He slowly succumbs to alcoholism and, as a result, is relieved of his position as school-caretaker. His final moral collapse is brought about when the school principal, whom Fak had entrusted with his money, cheated him out of his small capital. Fak dies because his health has been ruined by his drunkenness and because he could no longer bear the moral cruelty of his environment.

The novel derives its force not so much from the setting of its action, but from the psychological insight into the persons actions, and the description of landscape and environment. Society is not criticized in an insistent manner or with high-sounding words, but rather by a realistic depiction of the rural environment and its shortcomings. The author tries to make it clear how easily an innocent person can fall victim to calumny and damnation by the sheer weight of so-called public opinion however wrong or unjust this may be. Fak is unable to defend himself. He gets more and more isolated, a condition which eventually leads to his physical and moral collapse.

Apart from many imposing prose works, a large extent of versified poetry of outstanding quality, has been produced in the course of the last two decades. It must be emphasized here once again that the artistic talent inherent in the Thais finds an adequate expression in versified poetry in a more differentiated way than in all the genres of prose writing.

The wealth of poetic works and the number of poets is so great that nothing short of a monograph could possibly do justice to the evolution of Thai poetry even during so short a period as two or three decades. What is more, the linguistic interpretation of many verses in modern poems alone is so difficult to penetrate—we know of parallel difficulties in western literature—that it is almost impossible for a single author to give more than a survey in general outline.

What the author of this study aims at, in the frame of the present introduction to Thai literature, is not merely to state names and titles in a cursory manner but rather to give an idea of the present state of the evolution of Thai poetry by means of selected examples.

In current literary discussions in Thailand, mainly in Bangkok, the name of **Sonthikan Kancanat** is mentioned only marginally. Today, issues other than those dealt with by this poet, have emerged in the foreground. Moreover, the manner of his diction is no longer regarded up-to-date. Sonthikan ventured to express in his verses his innermost troubles in an idiosyncratic fashion. Without any inhibitions he laid open his inner feelings to the public. In so doing he marked a turning point in Thai lyrics. His friends and colleagues had sensed, already in his life time, the uniqueness of his work and personality. In their funeral orations we recognize even today the profound dismay which every single one of them felt when they heard of his demise in Bangkok. The following notes are based on their reports:

Sonthikan Kancanat was born in southern Thailand on August 3, 1932 and died in 1980.

The language used in his verses can be characterized as simple and unaffected and adequate to the frankness of his message. There are no vacuous phrases in his writings. In his utterances he takes a direct approach to the core of what he has to say. There are practically no embellishments or euphoric paddings.

In many of his poems Sonthikan tackles one of the gravest problems of Thai domestic policy. In spite of all 'rural development projects' promoted by the Bangkok government, their policy has so far failed to secure for the mass of small and medium-sized land owners a fair share in the economic boom of the country that has been going on unabated for many years.

The lot of the farmers is only one aspect—though a very weighty one—of the unbalanced social structure. According to Sonthikan, Thai society has become degenerate owing to 'a lack of ideals,' and because it is depressed by the capitalistic system 'since there is a division into "them", "that man there" and "me".' Sonthikan expatiates on this subject in his poem entitled 'He and He.'

Sonthikan's social criticism has, however, no political implications. He is not a messenger of salvation. Sonthikan's views are not narrowed in by misanthropic ideologies but, on the contrary, he is inspired by profound humanitarian ideals. To the sufferings of afflicted mankind he proposes the hope of 'a new life', a new world ruled by '(dhammic) law'. His creative work is crowned by poems whose titles already comprise a whole program, such as 'Life Aspiring to a New Heaven,' 'There is Still Hope,' 'At the End of our Wits, we Must Still Go On.' The poet does not behave like a prophet or a dreamer. He notices the shortcomings brought about by men in their dealings with each other and in his verses he calls them by their names. ('Do not accuse me of being foolish and ignorant of the world'). Sonthikan is, however, so much aware of his own humanity that he does not make accusations. He is content with mere statements of social injustice. That is accusation enough. No one could dissuade him from his belief in an ideal—or 'the' ideal—and in almost hymned verses he calls upon his readers to strive for such ideals:

> 'Dearest, let us hasten to set up an ideal!'
> 'The ideal.'

> 'It is lofty, enlightened, what is dreamt of'
> '... .the circle of life is beautiful'

Sonthikan is not deterred by any supposed injustice and exhorts his reader to accept life as it is and to fight lawlessness and never give way to pressure.

> 'Even with sweat running down, we do not give up.
> To expand life as imagined.
> Go ahead with determination. Broaden and pave the way to happiness towards the end and before life takes leave of the world!
>
> 'I must keep going ....
> .... one day I shall regain my strength.
> I shall then say there is a 'Law', which is permanent.
> At the end of our wits, we must still go on.'

Even those who can gain only little from Sonthikan's verses must admire his human strength and his unshakable faith in the justice of resistance against 'lawlessness'. Notwithstanding all the precision of his phrases and the terse concision of his verses many of them ring out as jubilant hymns of hope:

> 'For the sake of your hope expanding, stand firm.'
> 'Bear pains by strength of faith and base hope on the purity of life'.

While still alive, the poet attained a prominent position through his poem, 'From the Cau Phraya to the Banks of the Mae Khong' and 'From the Banks of the Mae Khong to the Cau Phraya.' Both poems would probably not qualify to be included in an anthology set up according to strict rules of literary criticism. They are too superficial, sentimental and not very different to trashy hit songs.

The following poems from the collection *Khit Thueng Sonthikan Kancanat* may serve as examples:

> (I) Because of .... injustice
>
> With a pure and stainless heart I attract hope.
> For I strive to stand firm on faith, constant endeavor and affirmation.

Society however becomes degenerate—because of injustice.
Everyone tries to escape from his own anxieties.

Because men are so overweening, they are blind to life.
Because certain things. . . coerce them, they are proud and rash.
Because injustice is so powerful and overweening. . . !
Because men so surely follow the way of depravity.

Since a long time there is a total lack of ideals.
Since they turned away from law that guides the heart.
Since society exerts pressure forcing people down to the earth.
Since their life knows no law, justice is stamped out.

Because the system of capitalism pressures from all sides . . . !
Because there is scarcely any hope to preserve life.
Because divisions are made between 'them', 'the man there' and 'me',
    these classes
Because the voice of law and freedom is muted.

(VI) He and He

He drives a car, boasts of luxury, holds his head high.
He is conspicuous on the dancing floor, jesting to sweet melodies.
He lives in a high-rise building, obviously beautiful.
He is cheerful with his girl friend waiting for him.

His life is glamorous, ecstatic, he is held in high esteem.
He despises the mass of poor people at any time.
He splits people up into classes: 'I', 'that man there', 'you'.
He loses self-control, bragging without restraint, boosts himself up.

He is exhausted—however much, he does not give up.
He is covered with sweat, very poor, enduring the gloom.
He is pressed hard—so much so that tears are running.
He will call out and beg—beseech whom?

With his buffaloes he treads the soil in the extensive field,
Since dawn already. The buffalo goes in front, he carries the plough on his shoulders.
He carries on with endurance, with the strength of his heart.
Because he is a Thai—but only a Thai farmer.

'He' of this group, does he exist at all? Who sees him?
He is in the position of a slave, devoid of all happiness.
He hears others say: 'rice' is valuable.
He, the farmer, is poor as ever—and has to endure oppression.

(LII) Waiting

When the moon, near the horizon, wanes in the dark sky
It is as if my heart would wither, weak and confused.
Soft songs continually pervade the air.
To take leave. Thinking with a moan of nothing else but the end.

The rich scent of flowers comes as an excitement
as if by magic someone had conjured up the scent of entire gardens.
This indicates to me that you
came to remind me to sing songs to my fiddle.

There is emptiness all around, voids and deathly silence.
Very cool, fragile, fearing the night—or?
Life is fickle for a man waiting.
Waiting for the teasing voice of his beloved who disappeared.

I wish the wandering moon would reappear in the sky.
Songs should not be lost, the voices should not vanish!
Enticing scents reach a man waiting!
You, dearest, are always welcome to sing.

All those who separated should come back,
Come and sing heavenly songs in turn.

Here in the open air amidst exciting and enchanting scent.
In praise of dreams of a glittering sky, of light and the moon.

My senses are fully awake seeking time to think of you,
who are comparable to
life's happiness. You as a friend are the happiness of the home.
You come as a friend—to unite with the waiting lover.

(LIII) Oblivion

Taking leave, meeting on the last day.
This suggests. . . 'the end of friendship, the end of remembrance,
the end of hope, the end of a hundred bonds of love
even between persons who were supposed to be forever attached to
each other

The glance of your eyes on that day intimated to me that
What was transient, forget it, it should vanish like a dream.
No desire for truth—for our bond of love
When in our life the day comes to part our ways'.

We separated a long long time ago.
I remember the glow in your eyes and feel depressed and empty.
The constant excitement of love has given way to indifference.
Love separated from life, the dream passed by like a child.

Oh your exciting, enticing scent!
I tasted, caressed you, kissed the strands of your hair,
Your ever-present tender scent excited me to praise you.
You are caught deep down inside me, I do not forget.

Enticing tender scent of your cheeks,
as if beauty herself would lay herself open, and one would be capti-
vated by it.
Love is confusing, to love means to be restless.
Surely it will get lost, disintegrate,—be indefinitely remote.

My thoughts turn towards a hope.
'Is there still a spark of love in you?
If you have forgotten the first deep-drawn kiss
I shall cease to follow you,—never ask again'.

Today's most popular Thai poet is **Angkhan Kalayanaphong**. He was born in southern Thailand in 1926 and has dominated Thai literary discussion for at least two decades—discussion related to poetry in general and of his works, in particular.

In Thailand, Angkhan enjoys an outstanding reputation as a draftsman, a painter, and a poet. He has won international recognition as a painter and graphic artist.

Here are the titles of some of his works: *Lam nam Phu Kradueng* (1969, 2nd impression 1973), *Nirat Nakhon Si Thamarat* (1972), and *Panithan Kawi* published in 1986. Anyone who sets out to read the poems of Angkhan is well advised to discard cherished old ideas about lyrical poetry: Angkhan's verses are like the footprints of a tiger, sharply outlined, of soft and velvety beauty, but menacing. Once under their impact no one can manage to step aside and adopt a non-committal attitude. Angkhan's verses are like cornerstones that compel you to stop short. He introduces into Thai poetry dimensions and qualities hitherto unknown. The following paragraphs will give the reader a few hints. But, first of all, one's attention must be drawn to things that are not, or not immediately, apparent from the cursory summaries of the individual poems.

(a) Angkhan was the first poet who dared to make use, in poetic texts, of unusual words and phrases to express what was on his mind. This is the most striking new formal criterion. It also implies the out-and-out use of Anglicisms wherever appropriate.

(b) For the right interpretation of his poems it is important to know that words like 'divine', *thiph(aya)* and 'eternal', *atam*, are not missing in almost any of his poems. Angkhan is virtually imbued with the idea of a divine and eternal world and poetry. He is certainly aware of his social environment, but only on a secondary plane. On the other hand he is obsessed with ideas of an elementary Buddhism of popular appeal.

(c) Depending on such ideas is the meaning he attributes to the concept of 'time.' Time for him is a tyrannical power which must be overcome like the 'flux of time', *krasae san (wela)*, time which 'flows', *lai* or 'melts', *lalai*. His poem shall surpass time and last for ever.

(d) Not one of the Thai poets before Angkhan could give expression to such a deep insight into nature as Angkhan does. Nature to him is creative force *per se* and his lyrics are at their best in poems praising nature—when he is virtually one with nature in body and soul.

(e) His frequently uttered strong aversion against women,—or one woman in particular— are probably documented through the history of his life. His complaints about a deficient human willingness or incapacity for love are also connected with it.

The critical capacity of Angkhan reached its peak in the long poem 'Bangkok-Thailand.' It can be said without reserve that this poem constitutes a unique critical damnation of Thai society in the seventh and eighth decades of the present century. Without the least attempt to gloss over the true situation everything is subjected to harsh and merciless criticism: government institutions, private patterns of behavior, the sciences, the notorious Thai entertainment industry, as well as bosses of industry, and politicians. A poem of this kind is really an all-round clearance, until now unheard of in Thai literature. With poems such as this, social criticism, as a new element, has taken root in Thai poetry. Objections to the effect that such criticism could be regarded as being somewhat exaggerated does not detract in any way from its validity. Hyperbole, as is well known, is a legitimate, nay necessary, stylistic medium in art.

Angkhan does not merely intend to accuse but rather to provoke as a poet and a citizen. From a poetic view-point the provocation of these verses lies in the fact that they are expressed in what is known as *lam nam*. Cognizance must be taken that 'Bangkok-Thailand' is a *lam nam* poem, a 'song' representative of a new age.

Bangkok—Thailand

(1) Bangkok—rubbish, corpses, fragment of the gods.
In the holy city people congregate to commit evil.
Negroes and foreigners hope to sponge on whores.
They make love in coffee-shops.

(2) Hippies shout hi hi, hae, hae,
Their songs are projected as far as Chieng Mai in Siam.
At the university they study in like manner.
Niggers are lousy but play good music.

(3) The teachers' college is obsessed and organized with blind eyes.
Eagerly striving for university status, big and crammed to capacity.
Masses are on the move to pester the earth.
Eagerly striving for a doctor's degree, nasty characters.

(4) Engineers conceal their cunning tricks like dinosaurs.
Drink themselves silly, bawling they drink themselves to death.
The teachers—neither one thing or the other—do the same.
They encourage evil to spread and become overpowering.

(5) The study of science and the arts is abandoned.
In feverish madness they embark upon carnal desire, on scandals and yearning,
Capable only of boxing with vigor,—unaware of things —
Turning in a circle of ignorance.

(6) Assiduous students exert themselves—in massage parlors.
Learning has exhausted them, they suffer, are tired and tremble.
They hire any depraved, dirty faded whore
looking for sweetness like cockroaches and believe themselves great men.

(7) The beauty queen is smelly with putrefaction, her brain is feverish.
She must participate in competitive shows bragging about her beauty.
Loud acclaim—she is Miss Universe—and become rich
by selling her virginity.

(8) Magicians are the maidens of Bangkok with soft brains.
In hot temper they quarrel with each other about the pleasure of inorgiastic sex.
Greedily they buy any available 'prick' of strong boxers.
So that they can fight for Thailand with enthusiasm.

(9) There is cheating in cock-fights—round about the national flag.
Nevertheless, they manage to appear as countless good people.
All others are lousy, of no worth on earth.
Just a trick, bloody shit, and really a thousand fold shame.

(10) Hill-tribes commit the sin of destroying the woodland.
    The forests have turned into waste-land, tremendously hot.
    Chinese together with Thais cooperate in its destruction.
    The tree trunks are rolled into saw-mills—I am disgusted. . . .

In this strain the poem continues in twenty-one more verses. Nothing is left unscathed.

Small Notes

(1) I wait at the owl's rock, buy glutinous rice
    and ask for some *Pla ra* for eating.
    Wrapped up tightly in leaves it is hot emitting a lush scent.
    Good for the gastric juices,—something,—or other?

(2) Keeping provisions of food to feed others —
    Especially if someone should be hungry.
    Partake of alcohol when the belly calls in agony.
    Buying with greed: fish and dear old brandy—just for tasting.

(3) I need no explanations from anyone.
    As a humble person I learn quickly.
    I know the right method how to learn things.
    I have also mastered the science of satisfying my belly.

(4) Motor-cars honk noisily—trah, trah —, as if mad
    Negotiate bends in a showy manner, swirling up dust
    a car-load of friends,—people as if made of wood.
    Driving with purpose—tilting over—crushed to death.

(5) This is normal for wild animals driving cars.
    How could they do away with their bad habits?
    Thundering, barking and trumpeting: painful to the ear and burning the liver.
    There is nothing to repair. It all ends up in an evil and mean manner.

(6) Automobiles soar up high—near the realms of death.
    Swerve, tremble, shake, fly as far as Sithan.
    And back again—very slowly—must cross waterways
    dried out like water soaked in sand.

(7) That is why Thailand is so beautiful.
    Evil is done, the open forest is killed.
    The dense jungle is thoroughly destroyed
    Until all streams have dried out.

The central theme in Angkhan's view of the world, the question of 'What is time,' is dealt with in three connected poems, in No. 40 (from a cyclus 'Certain offerings made to every age'). What kind of offerings? They are enumerated in detail, line by line, and contain in a nutshell Angkhan's entire world-view. The poem figures, therefore, among the most significant of all his poetic works.

Making Offerings to Every Age

(1) To take the land and people and join them into a chain.
    To give to splendid divine wisdom still more radiance.
    To get wrapped up in a view of the world bright as a rainbow,
    and spread it then all over heaven and earth.

(2) To see things as they really are, eternal infinite time.
    To be experienced in what is actual, above the value of heavenly
        dreams.
    The idea leads to the true core and
    brings forth the strength for a golden earth.

(3) To forget the meanness of non-humans.
    To create the elements of perfect purity, darkness vanishes.
    To know yourself in the right way.
    Quite clear and to appreciate the value of truth.

(4) To build and create more than heaven. I have made my choice.
    This is a task of gigantic divine benefit.

To check sin and evil with wisdom and expiate them.
To elevate the wonderful things as an offering to the soul.

(5) To learn assiduously in order to know what is what.
To penetrate all earthly things with intelligence,
and begin then to unlock a higher world, the universe.
To get an insight into all things, also those incomprehensible.

(6) To see the true value, to shed light into every corner of life.
To make sweet offerings to every age.
To be a wishing crystal for every heart,
a big one to contemplate ideas.

(7) To collect then the images of those wonderful ideas,
to create non-images that are above truth.
Bright blessings, radiant wonderful powers
bring forth an age of the golden discus everywhere.

(8) This age is to raise up low non-humans.
To raise their value by new wonderful elements
for a world of peaceful calm of the best kind.
To elevate the age of blood, enraptured wild tears.

(9) To bow to the vision of the bodhisatta
serving him for the consummate benefit,
to inaugurate an age of shiny creatures.
To proceed towards a golden age of the universe.

'Oh, I do not imagine the forest like that' is an unique hymn to the beauty of the forest which is a 'divine park.' (5) The poet's imagination and intuition are even transgressing reality:

(6) This day is the truth of many a world:
Magic casts a spell on heaven, lust and women.
The soul floats slipping away with songs
resting in solitude in the vast Himalaya.

'The soft pure air,—an eternal dream,' (7). And further on: Nature is forever innocent. 'plants do not know of revenge, wrath, anger,' and are beyond moral categories (19) peter out and sacrifice themselves (20). The poet's anathema against his own people is very harshly expressed here: 'Thailand in particular is in a very bad way' (25) with regard to the destruction of woods and parks.

(1) Oh, I do not imagine the forest like that
so deep, so beautiful, everything so special.
It pertains to dreams that are beyond truth
and I leave my soul in Phu Kradueng.

(2) Dense woods in dense forests; slowly
The rays of half a day mix with the night.
Strange atmosphere causing admiration
Loneliness up to the clouds, stillness and beauty.

(3) Rays of gold play upon, penetrate the tree-tops
rays displayed in stripes, the brightness of the sun.
I stretch out my hand drawing down clouds mixing them with brandy.
This is supreme happiness.

(4) The realm of plants so clean and tenderly flattering in the wind,
gradually mounting, they hide the wood like a curtain.
Soft moss hidden between rock and crevices.
All this the creation of heaven, so fascinating.

(5) The scenic setting of the wood in divine park land.
Whispering: heaven and earth. How can we believe it?
Like from a flute the tunes of birds rise in the forest.
The chirping of cicadas, after that silence.

(6) This day is the truth of many a world.
Magic casts its spell on heaven, lust and dreams.
The soul floats slipping away with songs.
Resting in solitude in the vast Himalayas.

(7) Tired I lie down near a rocky garden.
 The soft pure air—an eternal dream.
 Winds waft scent and sweetness
 excitedly glad soul over gained insight.

(8) Sweet scent of the flowers of prosperous trees
 Thriving under a peaceful sky and white clouds.
 Blossoming luxuriously, moving gently, of brilliant luster.
 A host of petals, stars in new-fallen dew.

(9) A heavenly hand divides the divine element of the air.
 The realm of plants is cheerful and in admiration as desired.
 Every season, every age is so beautiful.
 Assist and support each other lovingly!

(10) Some months of the year are designated for dryness.
 Causing difficulties and sorrows for all things.
 Patience even in face of need.
 Be quiet in expectation of death.

(11) Or should they complain and beat the evil and the wind?
 A bad omen is certainly followed by good fate.
 After April follows the rainy season of a future sky providing
 water. That is what is endeavored.

(12) The lofty trees do not think of reward for the scent of their blossoms.
 They are all disposed to give away also to this world.
 Men kill the wood because they venerate money as in all the world.
 The wood will not accuse them of viciousness by a single word.

(13) It is not obsessed with greed to make profit.
 Has a wide heart at all times, to be highly praised.
 Its dark greenness gives only shade
 as a service to all living creatures.

(14) It maintains the quality of the scents and their purity
 and its appearance and high dignity.

In it we are a far way, distant from shame and punishment of any kind.
It surrenders its life to the earth.

(15) The lofty trees contribute much to morals.
They should be infinitely lauded for it.
The trace of the ax kills. Blood runs in streams
Sawing, felling, sinking to the sands of the earth.

(16) Oh trees, open freely the clusters of your blossoms
in innocence, forgetting sin and malice.
It is difficult to seek tears which are shed.
To express longingly feelings of affection.

(17) In the blossoming season they all come forth beautifully.
Sweet scents as in divine realms.
There is scarcely any envy,
everything without a flaw.

(18) Who shall destroy this value which you do not curse?
You are able to kill at any time and remain calm and composed.
By the way, the trees are the handle of the ax which strikes
To destroy life in a cruel way.

(19) Plants do not know of revenge, wrath or anger,
they suffer things to happen, the killing by hand, the grave sins
Besides they protect against the hot poison of the sun
Giving shade as the head of the great lions with black hearts.

(20) You, trees, give the flattering pollen attended by scents.
You make this sacrifice again and again.
Do you ever respond angrily? You have accepted your fate
which is contemptuous of all that is beautiful.

(21) But troublesome are the murderers, the doers of future sins.
Greedy after money, they are blind to divine work.
Their hearts are black to large extent, instead of being honest and upright.
They have no breeding, are lawless.

(22) The trees try to preserve their lives
To save the world hoping to convert it into paradise.
They wait for the extinction of mankind.
Because non-human beings are cruel in every respect.

(23) Thailand in particular is in a very bad way.
Because of their (commercial) value parks are 'purified', i.e., destroyed
Man's blood is depraved, cursed and base.
His ancestors are swine and dogs. It is madness to say they are Thai.

(24) Mad after silver and gold, they destroy forests.
The trees are killed in the dense woods.
Indiscriminately they destroy every forest, so
as if trees had no hearts and souls.

(25) All forests are chopped down and destroyed to the very end,
because the barbarians feed on them like hungry spirits
destroying them incessantly.
They wait any minute to see dried up deserts.

(26) Because the human brute is cruel.
Poisonous, deceiving and greedy in the meanest manner
He will be put in a wooden coffin after death and
his corpse will be consumed by a fire fed by wood.

Phaibun Wongthet made a name for himself through his book *Maihet ruom samai*, 'Observations About the Present Age' which was published in 1978. A second, obviously unrevised, edition followed in 1983.

Phaibun was born in Pracinburi in 1952, in a town situated on the border to the eastern provinces, actually the poor-house of Thailand.

Influenced by his brother Sucit, Phaibun studied Thai literature of earlier periods together with the relevant historical sources (*phongsawadan and tamra*). His publications reflect his sound knowledge of, and familiarity with, the traditional literature of his country. Sucit Wongthet also ensured that Phaibun was familiar with contemporary literature and acquainted him with leading literary circles in Bangkok.

The Literature of the Present

Prior to *Maihet ruom samai* he had already published the following works: *Khuam khit si khau*, 'White Thoughts' in 2515 (1972) and *Kham prakat khong khon run mai*, 'Announcements of a Man of the New Age' in 2517 (1974).

The title of the poem *Maihet ruom samai* requires an explanation. The English translation of the Thai original renders its meaning only partially. *Samai*, admittedly, also means 'time' as a measurable transition from one state to another—as evidenced by Thai-Thai dictionaries—but in everyday spoken Thai and in literary usage *samai* has the meaning of 'age, epoch' and, in more extended use, 'basis, foundation, existence.' What meaning Phaibun attributes to *samai* is clearly shown by the content of the poem *Maihet ruom samai*.

Its twenty-four sections of various length are divided into 358 verses. The longest section is made up of thirty-six verses while the shortest comprises only four. Notwithstanding this apparent lack of system a definite plan can be made out from the arrangement of the individual sections. The poem begins with a threefold '...vow to make a sacrifice': to the heroes, to the teacher to the gods.

The introduction is in the form of a trinity like Buddha-Dhamma-Sangha or Brahma-Vishnu-Shiva. The choice of this arrangement is certainly not fortuitous. The introduction is followed by a 'Prelude' as in Thai classical stage plays. After the introduction the spectacle begins, apparently, with scenes from the *bot lakhon Ramakien*: Longka, the land of demons, and Ayutthaya, the city of Phra Narai, an incarnation of Rama. The polar points of the extensive epic are thus clearly indicated. In reality, however, it is not Ayutthaya of the *Ramakien* that is referred to here, but the capital city of Thailand, of old Siam, of about 1767 during the Burmese siege and its subsequent devastation. By city, *wieng*, are meant the estates located within the walls and the moat, the grand estates with the 'palace' in the centre. The topography is thus clearly indicated and the splendor and power of the rulers sufficiently praised. The sections headed by 'Money and Possessions,' 'Fields,' 'A Meritorious Spirit,' and 'Dark Times' deal in concrete terms with the situation of the people, their troubles, poverty and oppression. Verse 139 marks a break in the background setting. So far the action was set against the background of the *Ramakien* as projected until 1767 and even in the present. 'Tamarinds' and 'The Deaf-mute City', however, are sections focusing directly on the political and social life in Bangkok in about 1973. Still, Phaibun continues his narrative by reverting occasionally to scenes from Sunthon Phu's *Ruang Phra Aphaimani*, such as 'Sutsakhon' and 'The Ascetic'. While 'The Ascetic' expounds his precepts an 'Old Woman' sits in her hut waiting for the return of her dead son. The

'Didactic Lesson' draws the obvious conclusions from the situation of the 'Old Woman' and all those suffering like her, assessing the sum total like a manifesto of the age. The 'Didactic Lesson' is a summary of all preceding sections. The verse of the four sections that follow the 'didactic lesson' are but a detailed analysis of the 'Didactic Lesson'. The sections 'Prophesy' and 'I am at the End' are the finale and the colophon. Anyway, the structure of this part of the 'Observations about the Present Age' could be seen from such an angle. It is, of course, debatable whether such a view corresponds to the poet's intentions.

The poem 'The City' refers to Ayutthaya before its devastation, prior to the Burmese conquest. The high spirit born of anxiety, the unrestrained, in no way concealed, corruption that was rampant in the city in March and April in 1767 is implicitly documented in the accounts of the historical sources of the period. What the sources do not contain is presented by Phaibun: the predicament of those not at the top, either by rank or wealth, and were unable to avert hunger and death.

The City

>The Cau Phraya Kalahom is lucky
>sitting cheerfully on his bed ornamented with mother-of-pearl
>polishes his sword; arms in plenty.
>He makes sacrifices to the spirits, reciting magic incantations.
>
>The army approaches the city, this annoys him.
>He brandishes his sword—making a show.
>This sword, this iron is a ceremony.
>Citizens, fellow countrymen, for twelve *fuang*.
>
>Fighting according to the art of war, as required.
>Even brave, courageous soldiers are failing.
>Treacherous and very silly—in all towns —
>They sell swords and weapons in dejected mood.
>
>Some money for the spouse of the Kalahom.
>Some money to repair the hut.
>Some money for old vessels.
>Some money for a new tea pot.

The police look on with a smile: our share, please.
The government, rather upset, is helpless.
This money, please, for the child to buy a new mattress.
The finance minister is sad.

Oh please, I am aged.
Money, however, has its price irrespective of age.
The sale of this sword brings in cash.
If you sell why not share the proceeds?

Drums sound noisily, hoho, more noise.
Hey you, why are you stinking?
And you others do not make such noise!
I do not see why my share should be only one *fuang*.

Mue Waen is brave, his heart is courageous.
One part is enough, it should be given him.
Min Lue, victorious many times, protests immediately.
What then, dear friend, shall be my share?

The sundry items are not sold free.
A sword, a *fuang* evenly divided.
Share out the money among you, this is all right.
This way or another—everything is right.

Of course, trust is placed in ministers.
They, are flattered, there is much talk.
Merchants haggle over prices until people are persuaded.
They exceed what is permissible, cheat the people.

My person and my things come first, at any rate,
A hog for a capon—this is a barter.
One man likes this meat, another something else.
Those on top violently exploit people by stealth.

The Burmese sit and laugh to their heart's content.
There is no need for them to kill, the Thai will die by themselves.

> In the afternoon gongs and drums strike the hour,
> monks and nuns hurry away.
>
> The sky is aglow with fire, crows shriek.
> At Wat Prathan the gold flakes off, it dilapidates.
> Chants no longer prophesy
> Whether the country will grow even hotter by the conflagration.

One of the highlights of the poem 'Observations About the Present Age' is the section entitled 'A Didactic Lesson.' From a purely linguistic point of view it is one of the most difficult passages of the Thai original. Some parts elude even clear interpretation and hence adequate translation. Some of the words used in it are not even lexically recorded in Thai dictionaries.

In the original Thai version the section is headed by *Tamnan* which, according to the Thai Academic Dictionary means 'an account about events that happened in the past,'—this again implies that the historic account depicts the results of past deeds or misdeeds. In the light of the basic sense of the word the present author's translation by 'didactic lesson' appears to be justified. It is also justified in the light of its content. The poet is primarily concerned with a permanently existing condition without any historical reference.

The world view of this 'didactic lesson' is presented in realistic terms of gloom. Instead of white dew there is only the stench of blood, and instead of gems only crumbs of sand and dirt. The flowers are not flowers of evil, however, evil corrupts the flowers. Man destroys nature and commits murders in barbaric ways as in primeval times. River and morass tell the didactic lesson, 258.3 (This is a highly poetic line). Eventually a hunt is initiated, 'hunters call their companions', and the slaughter is cautiously planned involving mathematics and astrology. Phaibun has no illusions about the course of events. The slaughter is one thing, it is another thing that 'the sun emits its rays in the sky' and 'birds fall to the earth in masses.'

> The flight of birds has come to an end.
> There are no soft voices ringing wistfully.
> Not a single bird rises skywards anymore.
> Heaven remains heaven, however
> man made it disappear. (265)

A Didactic Lesson

There is no dew spreading white.
There is nothing but the stench of blood for auction and sale.
There are no glittering clear gems.
There are but crumbs of sand and dirt.

While evil rises, fragrant blossoms drop
also Phikun blossoms, and fade away.
Peacocks fall, wandering about, and Khae and Khun
Camari, all in bloom, are corrupted and fade.

Thong Kwau drop in great profusion.
Green banana leaves stand athwart in anger.
They are destroyed, chopped off, in all places.
Nothing but loneliness was left and instability.

Tears are running, there is no help.
Helplessly everybody jumps and pushes forward.
Blood is streaming, besmirching the earth,
Painting the soil reddish and then deep red.

Dark are hollows and steps of the gables.
Wild shadows of murders are reflected.
Heads are chopped off necks at the place of execution.
Across the shoulders hang sharp knives.

Skin and flesh are perforated, wounded, stripped
Cut across and pierced, hair cut off.
Clothes torn,—rip rip —, the breasts slashed open.
Knives thrust in to the hilt, cutting the hearts.

Driven by pain jumping up, defending oneself.
Blood gushing forth, running and flowing.
Stabbing and stabbing again, dropping to the ground unconscious.
Roasting on fire, stamping and crushing under foot—this is action.

Fire rich in flames, light, burning.
Kicking, beating and raging, looking up in great pain.
River and morass give this didactic lesson.
The hunters call their companions to follow them into the forest.

There is dried food in weave baskets.
Time is calculated by magic to be auspicious for the deed.
Bamboo is pointed into incendiary arrows.
Bows are covered with poison as weapons.

Looking up into the sky.
Spreading paper to prepare the assemblage.
Reckoning, multiplying, dividing with pleasure.
The astrologer determines the most auspicious day.

Moving slowly, looking around, crawling
along the pass-way in the mountains.
The sun emits its rays in the sky.
Birds rushing to and fro in swarms.

The hunter in position on his raised hide, draws the bow, the signal.
Bow beside bow, many, shooting aimlessly.
The birds are perched on the trees
in flocks together,—fall to the ground in masses.

They fall to their death,—almost all of them
the wooden weapons and spears also fall.
The rocks at the foot of the hills are besmirched with blood.
White pigeons spread their wings to escape.

Bows covered with poison are drawn.
There is hissing, nothing is left, everything dead.
Fires kindled with hay,—roasting and feeding.
There are no birds anymore, the forest is empty.

The flight of birds is at an end.
There are no soft voices singing wistfully.
Not a single bird soars skywards anymore.
Heaven remains heaven, however man made it disappear.

Born in 1940, **Nauwarat Phongphaibun** has hitherto published extensive work. Besides prose his titles include lyrical writing winning him recognition and fame. He was awarded the much sought-after SEA-Write-Prize in 1979 in recognition of his collection of poems titled *Phieng khuam khluan wai* or 'Mere Movement'. 'Mere Movement' has been divided into two parts by the poet. In defiance of what is usual, Nauwarat places his later poems at the beginning of this collection. The date of reference is pointedly 14 October, the day on which the student revolt was crowned with victory by the forced resignation of the Prime Minister and his hated deputy Praphat. The reference to a certain historic event is not accidental, but could be interpreted as a political credo.

'Mere Movement' is a poem of ten verses written in terse and precise language. In words comprehensible to every reader it describes a situation foreboding disaster. Nature and man are weighed down by oppression. But the poem also promises hope, even though hesitantly (3) 'there is a way out.' The first line in verse 6 should be taken literally: 'Emptiness or forty years, a vacuum all over the country.' Since the poem was composed in 1974, this would refer to 1934, almost to the year of the coup d'état of June 1932. The reference presumably means that in the view of people who want 'the victory of the people' (verse 10) too little change has been brought about in the political structure of the country. In the same verse, however, Nauwarat mentions, 'forty million years of immobility.' That is, he considers the misery of his age only as part of ever present universal suffering. Nature is perverted to such a degree that living creatures do not recognize it anymore (7). 'Only what is rotten is a sure thing/. However, the stillness of things brings forth something new . . . shining brightness' (8). 'The forward motion', by which Nauwarat understands the approach towards a new and better age, is attended by beauty and grace, it is 'no evil' (9). The report of guns is announced, admittedly, as a sign of victory (10). There is a total lack of 'pompousness' in this poem, and that is precisely what, among other things, determines its quality.

Nauwarat's diction and his poetic imagery are comprehensible to everybody who can read Thai.

Mere Movement

> The eagle briskly spreads its wings in the scorching sun.
> Tempers the heat of blazing rays emanating from above.
> Gentle rustling of leaves —
> You know the wind is veering.
>
> Only slight ripples, a glistening tremble.
> Indicating the water is clear, not a mirror.
> A timid hint in the eyes of the partner.
> And you know there is a heart in this breast.
>
> The chain blocking the door torn to pieces.
> The voices of sadness, of distress are loud.
> Pale light penetrates from somewhere.
> Yet you know there is a way out.
>
> The hand, a clenched fist wet with sweat.
> Not like blood, is aware,
> Exhausted, when to strike,
> feeling the sense of goodness and malice.
>
> Nervous fingers betray
> The hidden strength, it is obvious.
> The roots of grass split rocks, divide them
> and their dignity shines through,
>
> Forty years emptiness, a vacuum all over the country
> and forty million years immobility.
> Earth became sand, trees became rocks, even that broke asunder.
> Extinguished and sleeping everything, even eye and heart.
>
> Birds in the sky do not perceive the sky,
> fish in the water unaware of water.

The Literature of the Present

> Rainworms unaware of earth,—how could they be aware!
> Sightless maggots know only of dirt.
>
> Hence: what is rotten is a sure thing.
> However, the stillness of things brings forth something new.
> One day things rotting in the morass will bring forth,
> bright light. Lotus blossoms are admirable.
>
> And then moving forward—quite openly —
> Is grace and beauty, no evil.
> It might be dull, dim and dark.
> However it begins to take shape, it is a beginning.
>
> Hearing the bold vibrant sound of drums.
> You know another holy feast day is approaching
> When guns ring out in the provinces
> You know the people will be victorious.

One of the best known of Nauwarat's poems is the 'White Squirrel.' Found within the volume *Phieng khuam khluan wai* this poem is most lyrical and comes close to what is known in German as 'Stimmungslyrik', emotional poetry. However, in the 'White Squirrel' Nauwarat does not merely play with beautiful words reflecting the lyrical ego, but rather considers the poem to be a parable. The futile scurries of the squirrel stand for the abortive attempts of the Thai under military dictatorship.

White Squirrel

> From tree-top to tree-top, far away
> Hesitantly scurrying high up and low down.
> These are the ways and paths you follow
> This is reality as you know it.
>
> Who caught you, put you in a cage?
> The straight paths which were yours in freedom
> are nowadays designed by coercion.
> They have been restrained to a circuit in the cage.

Your far ways have been reduced to small circles,
your long ways have been shortened.
And there you run all day
turning, twisting quickly round by round.

What is it that you look for, little squirrel?
Exploring the paths, trails and cavities?
Or are you a well known actor
admired for turning in circles in a cage?

These are not the long tree top ways;
Just turning around is not a long journey;
Turning round about is not the Middle Path.
What do you long for, what else to do?

Have you found out yet, little squirrel?
The ways you want to follow
The long paths you have lost?
Who caught you and put you in a cage?

21 September, 2518 (1975)

The poem 'Brutal Pleasure' is a masterpiece of poetry. Words, images and ideas are woven into a fine web. Every single verse of this poem is evidence of high art. The 'Brutal Pleasure' is in fact the feeling gained from insight into the omnipotence of nature. The last verse, as an antithesis to the preceding ones, clearly sets out the brutal concomitants attending on pleasure.

Brutal Pleasure

Touched by the blue of the sky my dream is colored.
I surround the edge of my heart which is the basis.
Shining white rays of the moon illuminate the world,
flatter and caress the fertile soil the long rays of heaven.

Pray, the redness of the shining sun,
by which the dazzling rays are clearly dabbed.

Color of the flesh of deer in a fine web
delicately interwoven in cloth which covers the skin.

The echo of singing birds borne in a waft of air.
Twittering and whispering many a song at intervals
Glistening violet hues of blossom-clusters
evoke admiration the lively color
Bright orange alternates with white color.

Bringer of gladness, the eyes of young women to be deeply adorned.
Glittering gems fall like scales flashing many facets.
Love is a drop, the rays of stars as decoration.
Colors are silent, repress language. Every detail of art is precise.

Rock and forest pretend there being only deficiency
Greenness kills cruelly, destroys.
The colors of the night swallow the world.
The Universe is annihilated, deserted right to its end.

Khomthuon Kanthanu (born in 1950) became known above all through his volume of poems *Samnuek khabot*, 'Meditating on the Revolt' published, according to the imprint on the book, in 1980. Prior to this the poet had already published other texts, poetry and prose. Further works by him were published subsequent to 1980. Initially a revolutionary poet, Khomthuon has now become a resigned spectator.

The content of the collection of poems 'Meditating on the Revolt' does justice to its title. It has political implications to a large measure. Some poems refer to topical events of day-to-day politics; Khomthuon is not afraid of tackling such themes. To him they are obviously the only possibility to cope with real life seeing that in our time everything is more or less political. Moreover, all of Khomthuon's publications are imbued with a strong sense of social involvement.

Four poems have been given the same title. 'Verses of the year 2522' which corresponds to 1979 in the Christian era. The present author does not know what made the poet refer to this particular year. This was the year in which parliamentary elections were held, General Kriengsak Chomanand became Prime Minister, and Vietnam began to invade Cambodia.

In the field of domestic policies the period was characterized by a certain easing of tension owing to Kriengsak's multi-party government: those politically persecuted returned from the jungle or from abroad and the economy recorded a growth rate of 6.7 per cent.

A striking feature of all these poems is the play with various metres of traditional literature which even then were rarely used. 'Meditating on the Revolt'—composed in conventional metres —, in the mind of Khomthuon is surely not contradictory. In Thailand, even a revolutionary and socially involved poet will always remain a Thai aware of his cultural heritage. It must be made clear that in Thai poetics a certain content does not invariably call for a certain metre, except in very rare cases.

There is an inner coherence between the poems 'The Companion' and 'Radiant Sun,' (5) and (6). Both poems admonish 'young people' to be active, to increase performing acts of goodness and decrease performing acts of evil. Khomthuon realizes that perfection cannot be attained by 'theories' (5.3), but he does not state what kind of theories he refers to. His verses have a suggestive effect. No one reading his works can resist the highly developed sense of linguistic virtuosity. Khomthuon's language is without frills or flourishes, there are no expletive adjectives or circumlocutions. There is no verbosity in his style, yet he makes his statements clear with an air of strict gravity.

'Receiving a friend,' (7) what friend? He who is an 'university graduate with a diploma' ascending the social ladder, or he who is given to meditation, or to he who is poor? Khomthuon has a friend in mind for whom 'it is not too late to change his ways,' 'so that all men can eventually attain the age of justice.' Of identical content is the poem 'Plucking Stars to Brighten the Sky.' It is a song praising ideal manhood 'This is man' (9) and it is followed by poems in praise of fighters (10 pp.). In this part of the collection the theme of the verses is only slightly varied. This notwithstanding, Khomthuon's linguistic skill finds new forms of expression for each variation. The revolutionary pathos of his diction abates in the poem 'My Child' (16) which expresses the grief of a mother over the death of her child. Despite all the emphasis which he places on this sensitive subject the poet does not deviate from the level of his elevated diction and his endeavor to transpose specifically personal concerns and suffering on to a more abstract plane. 'We are like that' (17), demonstrates Khomthuon's view of history to which we can only assent considering the despair of the present age. In a number of further poems the poet depicts the depressed state of those who have no immediate influence on the course of events, 'laborers' for instance. He commemorates a single man, 'Camrat Muongyam' who lost his life in the actual fighting of the revolt, or he depicts the general menace with which everybody is faced through the 'host of spirits' in 'Not Used to Long Fighting.' None of these poetic creations are based on an ideology, and it is just this fact that gives such great effect to Khomthuon's analyses and accusations and makes them so convincing. A comparison should be made between these poems and 'The Voices of Women.' The poetic force of the latter is impaired by the fact that the tones used to drive home its essence are too strident. It is, therefore, artistically the weakest poem of the whole volume. The 'Song of Phaya Yio,' (1) and (2) is the squaring of accounts with the journalistic profession to which the poet himself formerly belonged.

'October' and 'Bloody October, Victorious October' have no immediate thematic connections. The first title refers to the student revolt of 14 October, 1973, the latter to that of 6 October, 1976 by which a totalitarian regime resumed power once again in Thailand—the cabinet headed by Thanin Kraivichien with all the consequences: censorship, elimination of trade unions and all 'suspicious persons' in public life. Three different meters are used in the poem 'October' and two different metres are used in 'Bloody October'. As mentioned above, there are no objective criteria to account for the change of metre. However, it cannot be dismissed that the poet had certain conceptions in mind that prompted him to choose one or another metre.

One of the clearest poems of the whole cycle *Samnuek khabot* as regards content and structure is 'The flag'. Which flag? The national flag? A red flag with various emblems or nondescript signs? From the poem, arranged in four sections, this question cannot be answered. Since, however, all four sections begin with the identical line 'In situations of emergency, inevitable, in the middle of the combat ....' the flag represents the symbol, or the torch, of the situation.

(1) The poem 'The flag' declares: 'The mass of dogs have hearts of slaves,' above them is the 'helmsman' who resists and assesses;

(2) In situations of emergency 'the mass of people are mad after power,' however, people with 'right thinking' ... assess the process of existence clearly;

(3) In situations of emergency 'the host of lackeys are bloodthirsty', others, however, 'preserve the ideal' and speak the truth;

(4) In situations of emergency reformers are far-sighted, for 'the combatants', however, 'the right things have a high price: actual fighting.'

The core of the volume are the last seven poems which all bear the same title 'Meditating on the Revolt.' The first poem bears the subtitle 'Fare warning,'—a warning that is not addressed to mankind globally, as might be expected after the preceding expositions, but a warning addressed to every human being individually. In blatant realistic terms the poet depicts how 'a new man is born under the dismal sky' of a depraved domestic environment. Mother curses birth, father is an alcoholic. Such an environment burns and destroys like poison.' Such vulgar and repulsive impressions weigh upon the minds' of the young throughout their lives, 'Pain and grief are lasting' and—as in the last line—'the sensitive mind of pure children is irritated.'

'Meditating on the Revolt' (2) with the subtitle 'Yellow leeches' depicts the transition from boyhood to youth. The 'yellow leeches' are the Buddhist monks clad in yellow robes. Khomthuon vigorously denounces the perverted existence of the monks and their misuse of arrogated power which repels every right-thinking young man. 'They leave the temple and return to their f a t h e r l a n d.' (The last word is a literal translation and its use in this context is surprising. The word is only rarely used in Thai. In the present author's opinion it is a neologism modeled on western conceptual patterns). Apparently, Khomthuon intended to establish a clear mark opposed to his Buddhist environment.

The subtitle of the third poem is 'The freedom of the intellectual.' What the subtitle refers to is quite obvious . 'Freedom' in the understanding of the poet means the ability to liberate oneself from the low spheres of the superficial entertainment business of our time, to realize one's own poor material origins, and to recognize the student revolt of 14 October, 1973 as a beginning. This poem is immediately followed by the 'Return to the Vestiges of the Past' (4). 'The young men stamp their feet in a provoking manner,' they fight and come through. 'Increasing age changes life. . .'! But the revolutionary zest reverses 'Progress into retrogression.' The poem, 'Meditating on the Revolt' (5) is, in fact, ambivalent. In spite of the above-mentioned subtitle the ninth line reads: 'The meditation of the young upon the revolt // is getting more acute, stronger and more joyful.' And, 'Idle old age // suddenly regains agility. . . .' 'Meditating on the revolt' (6) is a poem commemorating one of the most barbaric events of modern history. The first line reads: 'There was great darkness at the end of the year 2519.' The parliamentary elections of April 2519 (1976) did not bring about the desired political stability. The left-wing student groups worked themselves up to verbal radicalism which provoked vehement reactions from right-wing nationalistic factions. In 1976 political murders became the order of the day. Eventually, things came to such a head at the beginning of October 1976 that a veritable orgy of brutality was triggered off. Students were lynched by students—supported by police—beaten with clubs and burnt alive. Part (7) of the cycle 'The promise to mankind' is a personal confession of Khomthuon 'to abide by the law,' 'to do away with all that is base—and even to sacrifice one's life for it.' This final part of the poem is couched in words not entirely devoid of pathos.

Verses (from the year) 22 (Part 1)
Rai dan about the present age

> Misfortune and disaster
> until the year of famine
> fed up to your back teeth
> in the year 2522 of the Buddhist era.
> Deserted the whole of Thailand
> everybody living in abject poverty
> depressed and oppressed.
> Too much blood spilled.
> Sweat running down,
> maimed limbs, broken bones.
> Everything mixed up profusely
> for the belly of the three greedy demons,
> also for the swarm of vermin,
> which follow them sucking their marrow,
> dumb and blindly like mad.
> The towns are pale and pallid
> through knives, lances and guns.
> There is violent coercion and menace
> to form groups,—whoop!
> Prices are soaring heho —
> at the discretion of those in command
> like hellish fire.
> This however is hidden, comes from a deep abyss.
> People shed tears, those speaking out,
> will have to suffer if acting openly
> if contradicting, they will be killed;
> if courageous, they will be arrested.
> They suffer many pains, their hearts break
> without justice and without a voice

for discussion.
According to the law of the jungle, they are dispersed in every direction.
People in unbearable grief.
The gap between generations is getting wider and wider.

This is Man

This is man: glorious, tall and big,	valiantly fighting evil.
This is man sacrificing himself for an ideal	his self and his heart.
The great ocean lying before him as a barrier	he will overcome it and resist.
Great dangers lying ahead,	he will fight not flee.
All men assail those of evil intent	who are depraved and shameless
All men support the theory	of permanent revolution
With great strength	they do not abandon this purpose.
For the best world view	is their guiding light.
Men proclaiming freedom	victoriously overcome the law of destiny.
Men beheading injustice	cause the evil ones to die.
This is like the mighty beating of waves	which demolish everything, This is true.
Who dares to oppose the people	so heavily oppressed?
The boat of men will reach its goal	with gigantic force
The ways are open	being purged of law breakers.

Bibliography

Anderson and Mendiones, eds. *In the Mirror, Literature and Politics in Siam in the American Era.* Editions Duang Kamol, Bangkok 1985, 303 pp.

Anuman Rajadhon. *Thai Literature & Sawasdi Raksa.* (Thai Cultural Series n.3) Bangkok 2499 (1956). 16 pp.

———. *Thai Literatures in Relation to the Diffusion of her Cultures.* Bangkok 1961

Bidyalankarana, H.H. Prince. The Pastime of Rhyme-making and Singing in Rural Siam. *JSS XX,1.* (1926). pp. 101–127

Bidya, Prince. Sebha Recitation and the Store of Khun Chang Khun Phaen. *JSS XXXIII, 1*, (1941) .pp. 1–22

Chitkasem,M. The Emergence and Development of the Nirat Genre in Thai Poetry. *JSS LX, 2.* (1972). pp. 135–168

Chongstitvatana,S. *The Nature of Modern Thai Poetry.* Phil. Diss. School of Oriental and African Studies, London 1984

Coedes-Archaimbault *Les Trois Mondes Traibhumi Brah R'uan.* BEFEO vol. LXXXIX, 1973

Dhaninivat, H.H. Prince Siamese Versions of the Panji Romance, *India Antiqua* (1947). pp. 95– 101

Egerod,S. *The Poem in four Songs—A Northern Thai Tetralogy*—Phayaphrom, Lund 1971. 203 pp.

Gerini, .G.E. On Siamese Proverbs and Idiomatic Expressions *JSS I.1.* (1904) pp 11–168

Gühler, U. Über Thai Sprichworter. *JSS XXXIV, 2.* (1945). pp. 97–144

Hartmann, A. Das Bot Lakhon Ngo Pa des Culalongkon. *NOAG (Nachrichten der Ges. für Netur- u. Völkerkunde Ostasiens)*, 104 (1968), pp. 57–75

Bibliography

Ingersoll, F.S. *San Thong - A Dance Drama from Thailand.* Rutland, Vermont and Tokyo 1973

Nollon, C. *La vie du Poète Sunthone-Bhou*, Rougerie 1959

Prem Chaya, Prince *The Story of Phra Abhaimani*, Chatra Books. Bangkok 1952 141 pp.

———. *The Story of Khun Chang Khun Phaen.* Two vols. Chatra Books. Bangkok 1955, 1959, 97, 197 pp.

Reynolds, F.E. and M.B. *The Three Worlds according to King Ruang, A Thai Buddhist Cosmology*, University of California, Berkeley 1982

Rosenberg, K.L. *Die traditionellen Theaterformen Thailands von den Anfängen bis in die Regierungszeit Rama VI.* MOAG (Mitteilungen d. Ges. F. Natur- u. Völkerkunde Ostasiens) Bd. LIV. Hamburg 1970. 485 pp.

———. *Die Epischen Chan-Dichtungen in der Literatur* Thailand. MOAG Bd. LXVII, Hamburg 1976, 486 pp.

———. *Die Geschichte der Kaki — Ein Jataka-Stoff und seine literarische Bearbeitung in Thailand and Kambodscha.* MOAG Bd. 83. Hamburg 1980. 109 pp.

———. *Das Bunnowat kham chan des Mönches Nak. OE (Oriens Extremus)* 17. 1/2 (1970), pp. 179–219

———. Bemerkungen zum buddhistischen Gehalt des Romens Phu Di von Dok Mai Sot. *NOAG* 118, (1975), pp. 41–51

———. Neun unveröffentlichte Theaterstucke (bot lakhon) aus dem alten Thailand. *NOAG* 129 (1981). pp. 30–79

Schweisguth, P. *Etude sur la littérature Siamoise* Paris 1951, 409 pp.

———. *Sunthon P'hu - Nirat P'hu K'hau T'hong, Essai des traduction litterale d'un poeme t'hai*, Limoges 1969

———. Les 'Nirat' ou poemes d' adieu siamoise, *JSS XXXVIII, 1.* (1950) pp. 67–78

Sibunruang, K. Khun Chang Khun Phen, *La Femme, Le Heros et la Villain Poeme Thai*, Annales du Musse Guimet. tome LXV, Paris (1960) 159 pp.

Wenk, KL. *Die Metrik in der thailändischen Dichtung.* MOAG Bd. XLII, Hamburg 1961, 160 pp.

——— *Die Ruderlieder -kap he rüö- in der Literatur Thailands*, (Abhandlungen fur die Kunde des Morgenlandes XXXVII, 4) Wiesbaden 1968, 179 pp.

———. *Phali teaches the Young, A literary and sociological analysis of Thai Poem Phali son nong.* (Southeast Asia Data Paper No. 18, Southeast Asia Programm, University of Hawaii). Honolulu 1980. XII and 218 pp.

_____. *Studien zur Literatur der Thai, Texte und Interpretatioinen.* MOAG Bd. LXXXIX, Hamburg 1982. 271 pp.

_____. *Studien zur Literatur der Thai Band II, Texte und Interpretationen von und zu Sunthon Phu und seinem Kreis*, MOAG Bd. 96, Hamburg und Bangkok 1985. 372 pp.

_____. *Studien zur Literatur der Thai Band III, Texte und Interpretationen zur Literatur des 19, Jahrhunderts.* MOAG Bd. 107, Hamburg 1987, 373 pp.

_____. *Studien zur Literatur der Thai Band IV, Ein Textbuch zur Literarur der Neuzeit.* MOAG Bd. 113, Hamburg und Niederglatt, 1989, 686 pp.

_____. Aus dem Reisetagebuch Culalongkon's, *NOAG 89*, (1960). pp. 14–24

_____. Some Remarks about the Life and Works of Sunthon Phu, *JSS 74.2.* (1986). pp. 169–198

For further reference *see*

Simmonds, E.H.S.
Tai Literatures: a bibliography of works in foreign languages.
Bulletin of the Association of British Orientalists, New Series Vol. 3 nos. 1 & 2, Dec. 1965

Index

A
Achin Pranchaphan   79
Angkhan Kalayanaphong   89
Anirut   10, 25
Anirut kham chan   8, 29

B
Boromakot   6, 16
bot lakhon   33, 59, 61
bot lakhon Inau   31
bot lakhon nai   25
Bot lakhon Ngo Pa   73
bot lakhon nok   25
bot lakhon nok Kraithong   32
Bot lakhon Raden Landai   59
bot lakhon Ramakien   31
Bot lakhon ruang Raden Landai   57, 58
Bunlua Kunchon   81
Bunnowat kham chan   24
Burathat   77

C
Cap tai   79
Cau Fa Thamathibet   16, 24, 59
Cau Phraya Khlang   27
Chaiyachet   31
Chat Kopchit   82
Chot Praphan   78
Chua fa   79
Chulalongkorn   66
Cindamani   11
Cotmai Cangwang Ram   77

D
Damrong, Prince   31, 76
Detchadison   56
Dhammapada   70
Dokmaisot   81

I
Inau   27, 33, 59

K
Kaki   30
Kamnoet Phlai Ngam   35
Kap ho khlong   12
Kap ho khlong than thong daeng   24
kham chan   55
kham klon   39

Kham Phiphaksa   82
Khamphun Bunthawi   82
Khang lang phap   80
Khau chue Kan   81
Khawi   31
Khawiphot Thamaphimon   77
Khit Thueng Sonthikan Kancanat   85
khlong   7
Khlong chaloem phra kiet Phra Narai maharat   12
Khlong Kamsuon   12
Khlong Kamsuon Si Prat   8
Khlong nirat Nakhon Sawan   12
Khlong ruesi dat ton   58
Khomthuon Kanthanu   109
Khon di thi lok mai tong kan   80
Khru Thep   77
Khun Chang Khun Phaen   33, 35, 40
Khun Phum   64
Khun Ram Kamhaeng   1
Khun Sue   78
Klai Ban   73
klon nirat   35
klon sepha   41
Koet pen ying   80
Konlabot kop ten sam ton   58
Konok Nakhon   77
kot monthienban   45
Kraithong   31
Kritsana Asokin   81
Kritsana son nong   55

L
lakhon   25, 29, 31
Lam nam Phu Kradueng   89
Levi-Strauss, Claude   39
lilit   7
Lilit Phra Lo   7
Lithai King   5
Long plai   80

M
Maha Montri   56, 57
Mahanak   24
Maharatchakhru   8, 10
Mahasurasinghanat   30
Mai Muang   78
Maihet ruom samai   98, 99
Malai Chuphinit   79
Manat Chanyong   79
Mom Ratchothai   67
Mongkut. *See* Rama IV

N
Nai Mi   56
Nang Nophamat   5
Nanthopanantha kham luong   24
Narai   6
Nauwarat Phongphaibun   105
Nen Klan   51
nirat   8, 35, 36
Nirat Inau   37
Nirat kap ho khlong than sok   24
Nirat Klaeng   35
Nirat muang Klaeng   46
Nirat Muang Phet   46
Nirat Nakhon Si Thamarat   30, 89
Nirat Nen Klan   37, 51
Nirat Phra Pathom   36, 39, 46
Nirat phu khao thong   39
Nirat Phu Khau Thong   46, 47
Nirat Suphan   46, 56
Nirat ti Phama   30

Index

Nirat Wat Cau Fa 46
nithan 35
Nithaya Natayasunthon 81
niyai 35

O
Ong kan chaeng nam 6

P
Paking nakhon haeng khuam lang 80
Pancatantra 27, 70
Panithan Kawi 89
Phaen din khong rau 80
Phaibun Wongthet 98
Phet Mongkut 27
Phet Phuong Mahachat 30
Phieng khuam khluan wai 105, 107
Phithayalongkon 77
Phleng yau chaloem phra kiet 64, 65
Phleng yau nirat phima thi din daeng 35
Phleng yau nirat rop phama thi tha din daeng 28
Phleng yau wa phra maha thep pan 57
Phleng yau wa phraya maha thep pan 58, 60, 61
Phra Aphaimani 33, 40
Phra Horathibodi 8
Phra Khlang 29
Phra Malai kham luong 24
Phra Narai 16
Phu chana sip thit 78
Phu di 81
Poromanuchit Chinorot 54

Prachum Phongsawadan 77

R
Rama I 28, 30
Rama II 29, 31, 32
Rama III 67
Rama IV 65, 67, 75, 76
Rama V 73
Rama VI 77
Rama VII 77
Ramakien 25, 27, 29, 44, 59
Ramphan philap 33, 47
ratchanukit 45
Ratchathirat 29
Raya 80
Rong Wongsawon 82

S
Sam kok 29
Sam Krung 77
Samakhiphet 77
Samnuek khabot 109, 111
Samuthakhot 10, 55
Samuthakhot kham 10
San-kuo-Chi T'ung-su Yen-i 29
Sawadi muang rae 79
Sawatdi raksa 49
Si Burapha 80
Si Mahosot 8, 12, 14
Si Prat. 8, 9
Sieng riek muang rae 79
Sifa 81
Sonthikan Kancanat 83, 84
Sot Kuramarohit 80
Sua Kho 10
Sunthon Phu 32, 56
suphasit 12, 49

Suphasit Phra Ruong   2, 70
Suphasit son ying   70
Suwani Sukhontha   81

T
Taksin   31
Taleng Phai   55
Thama Pricha   31
Thawathosamat   12
Thet Mahachat   7
Tohyanti   81
Trailokhanat   6
Traiphum Phra Ruong   31
Traiphumikhatha   2

U
Unarut   25

V
Vessantara Jataka   7

W
Wat Phra Chetuphon (Wat Pho)   67

Y
yaem   17
Yakhop   78
Yuon Phai   6